The Unspoken Kennedy Truth

Laurent Guyénot

ISBN : 978-2-9571704-1-8

In tribute to Michael Collins Piper (1960-2015)

CONTENT

Revised December 2021

INTRODUCTION

The title of this book is an ironic reference to the now classic book by James Douglass, *JFK and the Unspeakable: Why He Died and Why it Matters* (2008). It was my first serious reading on John Kennedy's assassination, and it determined my intense interest for the case. I loved it so much that I convinced a French publisher to translate it. It draws a great portrayal of John Kennedy's character, vision, and efforts for lasting peace, and it convincingly documents his struggle against the hawks of the military and intelligence establishment.

However, I now consider it to be misleading in its final verdict, for failing to mention crucial evidence. In that regard, Douglass's book is representative of the dominant school in JFK-assassination research. It has at least four huge blind spots: Johnson, Ruby, Angleton and — the biggest of all — Dimona.

Like other CIA-did-it theorists, Douglass almost completely exonerates Johnson, the natural prime suspect, and ignores the evidence of his complicity — nay, his central role. The obviousness of the fact that the conspirators acted with the foreknowledge that Johnson would cover them escaped Douglass. Naturally, authors blaming the CIA and Pentagon see no relevance in Johnson's extraordinary pro-Israel policy, which reached high treason when he authorized and then covered up the attempted Israeli false flag attack on the USS *Liberty*.

Jack Ruby, Oswald's assassin, is the most important man to investigate, short of knowing the identity of the real gunmen of Dealey Plaza. But Jacob Rubenstein — that's his real name — attracts little interest from mainstream JFK conspiracy theorists. They never mention his Irgun background, or that he repeatedly claimed to have "done it for the Jews." We are simply asked to assume, without evidence that he was a "CIA-connected" "Chicago mob functionary."

Like most investigators since the 1970s, Douglass recognizes James Jesus Angleton's central role in the fabrication of Oswald's fake incriminating background as KGB agent. But he ignores the two most important facts about Angleton: first, that Angleton's Counterintelligence Staff was a "CIA within the CIA," with extreme secrecy, tremendous power, and no accountability to anyone; secondly, that Angleton was also the exclusive CIA liaison with the Mossad, whose leaders honored him as a "friend you could trust," and "the biggest Zionist of the lot."

More importantly, Douglass highlights with great talent Kennedy's determination to abolish weapons of mass destruction, yet he never alludes to his standoff with Israeli Prime Minister David Ben-Gurion over the latter's determination to provide his country with a nuclear arsenal, a standoff that reached a breaking point at the end of 1963. Here again, Douglass's blackout is representative of a general trend. As Congressman Paul Findley dared write in March 1992 in the *Washington Report on Middle East Affairs*: "It is interesting to note that in all the words written and uttered about the Kennedy assassination, Israel's intelligence agency, the Mossad, has never been mentioned."[1] A laughable case in point is John Simkin's much consulted website Spartacus Educational and his 7,000-page encyclopedia on *The Assassination of John F. Kennedy*, from which any mention of involvement from Israel, the Mossad or the Jewish mafia is strictly banned.

From that viewpoint, the title of Douglass's book takes an ironic meaning: apparently, the truly "Unspeakable" is what Douglass doesn't speak about. The present book explores that unspoken Kennedy truth. It walks the road less travelled by JFK researchers, and it does so in the footsteps of Michael Collins Piper, the fearless author of *Final Judgment: The Missing Link in the JFK Assassination Conspiracy* (first edition 1994).[2]

This is a short book, not because I couldn't make it longer, but because I want to show that the case against Israel is straight-forward and easy to make. It stands firmly on a limited amount of indisputable facts, not on convoluted speculations and disputable testimonies. Besides, I assume that most of my readers will have read already a couple of books on the Kennedys, so that I don't need to repeat the basics.

I have tried to link the most significant facts into a clear and credible picture. I have focused on connecting the three big dots that are generally overlooked: Johnson, Ruby, Angleton. But first, I have connected John and Robert's assassinations, because the first key to solving both cases resides in their comparative analysis. Lance deHaven-Smith has remarked in *Conspiracy Theory in America:*

It is seldom considered that the Kennedy assassinations might
have been serial murders. In fact, in speaking about the murders,
Americans rarely use the plural, "Kennedy assassinations". . . .
Clearly, this quirk in the Kennedy assassination(s) lexicon reflects
an unconscious effort by journalists, politicians, and millions of
ordinary Americans to avoid thinking about the two assassinations
together, despite the fact that the victims are connected in countless ways.[3]

When both killings are mentioned together, it is generally
under the heading of the "Kennedy curse" — in which is included
the death of John's only son in 1999. That's a kabalistic smoke
screen. However, there is some cryptic grain of truth to it. If John
and Robert's lives and destinies are so entwined, it is because "the
Kennedy family is a clan, a tribe, a sovereignty, and a dynasty"
(Arthur Krock).[4] Filial piety for the patriarch was what kept the
Kennedys together and forged their destinies. Only by taking into
account this exceptional familial bond, and the controversial
political legacy of Joseph Kennedy, can one begin to understand
the true nature of the "Kennedy curse." There is no deep
understanding of JFK without knowing his father. Most JFK fans
ignore it, but JFK's mortal enemies have always known it.

CHAPTER 1
RFK'S False-Flag Assassination

Just after midnight on June 5, 1968, Senator Robert F. Kennedy, candidate to the presidency of the United States, was shot dead in the kitchen service pantry of the Ambassador Hotel in Los Angeles. He had just been celebrating his victory at the Democratic California primary, which made him the most likely Democratic nominee. His popularity was such that the Republican Richard Nixon stood little chance. At the age of 43, Robert would have become the youngest American president, after being the youngest Attorney General in his brother's government. His death opened the way for Richard Nixon, who could finally become president eight years after being defeated by John F. Kennedy in 1960.

Kennedy biographers have stressed the absolute dedication of Robert to his elder brother. Robert had successfully managed John's campaign for the Senate in 1952, then his presidential campaign in 1960. John made him not only his Attorney General, but also his most trusted adviser, even on matters of foreign or military affairs. What John most appreciated in Robert, he once told his friend Ben Bradlee, was "his high moral standards, strict personal ethics. He's a puritan, absolutely incorruptible."[5]

Laurence Leamer writes in *Sons of Camelot*: "Bobby had been the president's alter ego and protector. He could finish his brother's sentences and complete a task that Jack signaled with no more than a nod or a gesture. He had loved his brother so intensely and served him so well that within the administration it was hard to tell where one man ended and the other began."[6]

After 1963, Bobby was more than ever his brother's continuation. He neither possessed John's charisma nor his ambition. His brother's coat, which he had literally worn during his first months of mourning, was too big for him. When he sought to reclaim the White House in 1968, it was out of loyalty to his dead brother, and with the conviction that his own destiny was inseparable from John's, which itself had been determined by their father.

Robert knew that he was, in the eyes of millions of Americans, the legitimate heir to the murdered king — as well as his avenger. His public appearances led to displays of enthusiasm never seen before for a presidential candidate, and his total lack of concern for his own security only increased his prestige.

Given this exceptional bond between the Kennedy brothers, what are the odds that the two Kennedy assassinations were unrelated? Rather, we should start with the assumption that they are related. Basic common sense suggests that the Kennedy brothers have been killed by the same force, and for the same motive. It is, at least, a logical working hypothesis that Robert was eliminated from the presidential race because he had to be prevented from reaching a position where he could reopen the case of his brother's death. Both his loyalty to his brother and his obsession with justice made it predictable that, had he reached the White House, he would have done just that. But was there, in 1968, any clear indication that he would?

Did RFK plan to reopen the JFK investigation?

The question has been positively answered by David Talbot in his book *Brothers: The Hidden History of the Kennedy Years*, published in 2007 by Simon & Schuster. Robert had never believed in the Warren Commission Report's conclusion that Lee Harvey Oswald was the sole assassin. Knowing too well what to expect from Johnson, he had refused to testify before the Warren Commission. He was compelled to write a statement saying that he knew of "no credible evidence to support the allegations that the assassination of President Kennedy was caused by a domestic or foreign conspiracy," but he took care to have someone else sign it for him. When the Commission's report came out, he had no choice but to publicly endorse it, but "privately he was dismissive of it," as his elder son Robert Kennedy Jr. remembers[7]. To his friends who wondered why he wouldn't voice his doubt, he said: "there's nothing I can do about it. Not now."[8]

From November 22, 1963, Robert was alienated and closely monitored by Johnson and Hoover. Although still Attorney General, he knew he was powerless against the forces that had killed his brother. Yet he lost no time to begin his own investigation. A mere week after JFK's death, November 29, Bill Walton, a friend of the Kennedys, travelled to Moscow and passed to Nikita Khrushchev, via a trusted agent, a message from Robert and Jacqueline Kennedy. According to the memo found in the Soviet archives in the 1990s by Alexandr Fursenko and Timothy Naftali (*One Hell of a Gamble*, 1998), Robert and Jackie wanted to inform the Soviet Premier that they believed John Kennedy had been "the victim of a right-wing conspiracy," and that "the cooling that might occur in U.S.-Soviet relations because of Johnson would not last forever."[9]

Robert explored almost every possibility. He first asked CIA Director John McCone, a loyal Kennedy ally, if rogue agents within the Agency had anything to do with the plot. McCone knew nothing about it. In March 1964, suspecting a vengeance from organized crime, Robert contacted mobster Jimmy Hoffa, whom he had battled for ten years. A face-to-face encounter was organized between the two men on an airport runway, and Robert came out convinced of Hoffa's innocence. Robert also asked his friend Daniel Moynihan to search for any complicity in the Secret Service, responsible for the President's security.[10] And of course, Robert suspected Johnson, whom he had always mistrusted, as Jeff Shesol documents in *Mutual Contempt: Lyndon Johnson, Robert Kennedy, and the Feud that Defined a Decade* (1997). Already thinking of a way to regain the White House, Robert actually tried in 1964 to get Johnson to name him as his running mate, but lacked leverage. Johnson confided to John Connally: "I'm not going to let them put somebody in bed with me that'll murder me."[11]

Robert also contacted a former British MI6 officer who had befriended his family when his father was ambassador in London. This retired officer in turn contacted some trusted friends in France, and arrangements were made for two French Intelligence operatives to conduct, over a three-year period, a quiet investigation that involved hundreds of interviews in the United States. Their report, replete with innuendo about Lyndon Johnson and Texas oil barons, was delivered to Bobby Kennedy only months before his own assassination in June 1968. After Bobby's death, the last surviving brother, Ted Kennedy, showed no interest in the material. The investigators then hired a French writer to fashion the material into a book, under the pseudonym of James Hepburn. The book was published under the title *L'Amérique brûle,* then translated as *Farewell America: The Plot to Kill JFK.* "President Kennedy's assassination," the author concluded, "was the work of magicians. It was a stage trick, complete with accessories and fake mirrors, and when the curtain fell, the actors, and even the scenery disappeared."[12]

Robert had planned to run for the American presidency in 1972, but the escalation of the Vietnam War precipitated his decision to run in 1968. Another factor was the opening of the investigation by New Orleans District Attorney Jim Garrison in 1967. Garrison was allowed to view Abraham Zapruder's 8mm amateur film, concealed from the public until 1975. This film, despite evident tampering, shows that the fatal shot came from the "grassy knoll" well in front of the President, not from the School Book Depository located behind him, where Oswald was supposed to be shooting from.

When talk of the investigation began, Robert confided to William Attwood, editor of *Look* magazine, that he, like Garrison, suspected a conspiracy, "but," he added, "I can't do anything until we get control of the White House."[13] He refrained from openly supporting Garrison, whose investigation suffered a smear campaign and the mysterious deaths of his two main witnesses, Guy Banister and David Ferrie. His public support would only weaken his chances of election by construing his motivation as a family feud. But Garrison would later claim that Robert gave him a discreet message of support through a common friend, letting him know that he was going to "blow the whole thing wide open" when he is president. Garrison rightly feared that Robert would not live long enough, and thought that speaking out publicly might have protected him.[14]

In conclusion, there can be little doubt that, had he been elected president, Robert Kennedy would have done his utmost to reopen the case of his brother's assassination, in one way or another. This certainly did not escape John's murderers. Their best option was to stop him. This first conclusion is a sufficient reason to conduct a comparative analysis of both Kennedy assassinations, in search of some converging clues that might lead us on the trail of a common mastermind. Let us first examine the circumstances of Robert's assassination.

Sirhan Bishara Sirhan

Just hours after Robert's assassination, the press was able to inform the American people, not only of the identity of the assassin, but also of his motive, and even of his detailed biography.[15] Twenty-four-year-old Sirhan Bishara Sirhan was born in Jordan, and had moved to the United States when his family was expelled from West Jerusalem in 1948. After the shooting, a newspaper clipping was found in Sirhan's pocket, quoting Robert's following statement: "The United States should without delay sell Israel the 50 Phantom jets she has so long been promised." Handwritten notes by Sirhan found in a notebook at his home confirmed that his act had been premeditated.

That he had been moved by his hatred of Israel became the mainstream storyline from day one. Jerry Cohen of the *Los Angeles Times* wrote a front page article, saying that Sirhan is "described by acquaintances as a 'virulent' anti-Israeli" (Cohen changed that into "virulent anti-Semite" in an article for the *Salt Lake Tribune*), and that: "Investigation and disclosures from persons who knew him best revealed [him] as a young man with a supreme hatred for the state of Israel." Cohen infers that "Senator Kennedy . . . became a personification of that hatred because of his recent pro-Israeli statements." Cohen further wrote that, about three weeks before the shooting, Sirhan wrote in his notebook: "Kennedy must be assassinated before June 5, 1968," that is, Cohen notes, "the first anniversary of the six-day war in which Israel humiliated three Arab neighbors, Egypt, Syria and Jordan."[16] Cohen had gotten that information from Los Angeles Mayor

Samuel Yorty, who, within hours of the shooting, was able to reveal in a press conference the contents of Sirhan's notebook before it had even reached the LAPD.[17]

After September 11, 2001, the tragedy of Robert's assassination was rewritten and installed into the neocon mythology of the "Clash of Civilizations" and the "War on Terror." Sirhan became a precursor of Islamic terrorism on American soil. A book entitled *The Forgotten Terrorist,* by Mel Ayton (2007), purports to present "a wealth of evidence about [Sirhan's] fanatical Palestinian nationalism," and to demonstrate that "Sirhan was the lone assassin whose politically motivated act was a forerunner of present-day terrorism."

In 2008, on the occasion of the 40th anniversary of Bobby's murder, Rabbi Jeffrey Salkin wrote in *The Forward*: "One cannot help but note the parallel between Kennedy's assassination and the terrorist attacks of September 11, 2001. In both tragic cases, Arab fanaticism reared its ugly head on American soil, irrevocably changing the course of events in this country."[18]

The same day, Sasha Issenberg of the *Boston Globe* recalled that the death of Robert Kennedy was "a first taste of Mideast terror." He quotes Harvard professor Alan Dershowitz saying: "It was in some ways the beginning of Islamic terrorism in America. It was the first shot. A lot of us didn't recognize it at the time."[19] That Sirhan was from a Christian family was lost on Dershowitz.

The Forward took care to mention it, only to add that Islamic fanaticism ran in his veins anyway: "But what he shared with his Muslim cousins — the perpetrators of September 11 — was a visceral, irrational hatred of Israel. It drove him to murder a man whom some still believe might have been the greatest hope of an earlier generation. . . . Sirhan hated Kennedy because he had supported Israel."

For anyone familiar with Kennedy history, there is something suspiciously absurd in making the assassination of Robert Kennedy a crime against Israel. But let us, for the moment, take these declarations seriously, and let us try to understand what kind of anti-Zionist Palestinian "terrorist" was Sirhan Sirhan. While studying his case more closely, perhaps we can learn something about the very nature of that Arab terrorism that has now become a leitmotiv of the dominant narrative in our post-9/11 world.

Our first question is: Did Sirhan really kill Robert Kennedy?

Did Sirhan really kill Robert Kennedy?

If we trust official statements and mainstream news, the assassination of Robert Kennedy is an open-and-shut case: the identity of the killer suffers no discussion, since he was arrested on the spot, with the smoking gun in his hand.

In reality, a thorough review of the evidence leads to a different conclusion. I can only here summarize some key points. A detailed exposition of all the evidence presented at the trial and uncovered or declassified ever since can be found in two remarkable books:

- William Klaber and Philip Melanson, *Shadow Play: The Unsolved Murder of Robert F. Kennedy* (1997), revised edition, Macmillan, 2018;

- Tim Tate and Brad Johnson, *The Assassination of Robert F. Kennedy: Crime Conspiracy & Cover-Up: A new investigation* (2018), second edition, Lume Books, 2020.

Ballistic, forensic and eyewitness evidence shows that none of Sirhan's bullets hit Kennedy. According to the autopsy report of Chief Medical Examiner-Coroner Thomas Noguchi, Robert Kennedy was hit by three bullets, while a fourth went through his coat. All these bullets were shot from behind Kennedy: two of them under his right armpit, following an upward angle, and the third, the fatal bullet, a few inches behind his right ear, at point blank range. Dr. Noguchi reaffirms his conclusion in his memoirs, *Coroner* (1983). Yet the sworn testimonies of twelve witnesses established that Robert had never turned his back on Sirhan and that Sirhan was five to six feet away from his target when he fired. Moreover, Sirhan was physically overpowered by Karl Uecker after his second shot, and, although he continued pressing the trigger mechanically, his revolver was not directed towards Kennedy anymore.

By tallying all the bullet impacts in the pantry, and those that wounded five people around Kennedy, it has been estimated that at least twelve bullets were fired, while Sirhan's gun carried only eight. On April 23, 2011, attorneys William Pepper and Laurie Dusek gathered all this evidence and more in a 58-page file submitted to the Court of California, with a request that Sirhan's case be reopened. They pointed out major irregularities in the 1968 trial, notably that the serial number of Sirhan's pistol did not match the serial number of the pistol by which were test fired the bullets

compared with those extracted from Robert's brain.[20] Included in
the file submitted by Pepper and Dusek was a computer analysis of
a soundtrack recorded on a portable tape-recorder by reporter
Stanislaw Pruszunski during the shooting. The analysis,
commissioned by Brad Johnson, was conducted in 2008 by audio
engineer Philip Van Praag, who concluded

> that 13 shots, or more, were fired in the pantry during that brief
> five second period of time; that five of those shots were fired from
> a . . . direction opposite to the direction that witness accounts
> report as the direction in which Sirhan was firing . . . and that in
> two instances within those five seconds there were virtually
> simultaneous, or 'double' shots . . . In my opinion the conclusion
> is inescapable that there was a second gun fired by a second
> shooter during the shooting that resulted in the death of Senator
> Robert F. Kennedy.[21]

Paul Schrade, a Kennedy confidant who was behind Robert
during the shooting and received one of Sirhan's bullets, has long
believed there was a second shooter (he said so in a press
conference with Allard Lowenstein in December 1974). He
testified at Sirhan's 2016 parole hearing, and told him: "the
evidence clearly shows that you were not the gunman who shot
Robert Kennedy."[22] Robert F. Kennedy Jr. and his sister Kathleen
have joined Schrade and support the call for a reinvestigation of
the assassination of their father.[23]

The presence of a second shooter was mentioned by several
witnesses and reported on the same day by a few news outlets.
There are suspicions that Robert's real assassin was Thane Eugene
Cesar, a security guard hired for the evening. Cesar was stuck
behind Kennedy at the moment of the shooting, and some people
saw him draw his pistol.[24] Cesar's weapon was never examined,
and he was never interrogated.[25] Some witnesses, however, believe
that the second shooter was not Cesar, but another person who fled
the place immediately after the shooting, together with the famous
"girl in a polka dot dress" that at least twenty-five eyewitnesses
saw at the Ambassador Hotel in the afternoon or evening of June 4,
and that others saw running down the exit stairs after, laughing and
shouting, "We shot him! We shot him!"[26]

Even if we assumed that Sirhan did kill Robert Kennedy, a
second aspect of the case raises question: Sirhan seemed to be in a
state of trance during the shooting, and of disorientation just after.
George Plimpton, while struggling to restrain Sirhan, noticed that

he had "enormously peaceful eyes . . . In the middle of a hurricane of sound and feeling, he seemed peaceful." Randolph Adair, a police officer who took Sirhan to custody just after the shooting, said that "He had a blank, glassed-over look on his face — like he wasn't in complete control of his mind." When patrolman Arthur Placencia inspected his eyes with a flashlight, the absence of reaction of his pupils made him conclude that "he was under the influence of something."[27]

More importantly, Sirhan has always claimed that he has never had any recollection of his act. His memory stopped with having a coffee with a pretty girl (in a polka dot dress), and began again with his being choked after the shooting. Fifty years after the facts, he continues to declare: "I was told by my attorney that I shot and killed Senator Robert F. Kennedy and that to deny this would be completely futile, [but] I had and continue to have no memory of the shooting of Senator Kennedy." He also claims to have no memory of "many things and incidents which took place in the weeks leading up to the shooting."[28] Some repetitive lines written in a notebook found in Sirhan's bedroom, which Sirhan recognizes as his own handwriting but does not remember writing, are reminiscent of automatic writing: there is, for example, a whole page of fifteen repetitions of *"RFK must die, Robert F. Kennedy must be assassinated, assassinated, assassinated, assassinated,"* suddenly turning to *"I have never heard please pay to the order of of of of of."*[29]

Psychiatric examinations carried during Sirhan's trial by renowned psychiatrist Bernard Diamond have confirmed that Sirhan's amnesia is not faked. In their book *Shadow Play,* William Klaber and Philip Melanson summarize Dr. Diamond's conclusions in this way:

> He overcame his initial disbelief of Sirhan's claims of not remembering the shooting or the notebooks and began to search for explanations. He had hypnotized Sirhan on eight occasions and made some interesting discoveries. He discovered, first of all, that Sirhan was very easy to hypnotize. He discovered signs that Sirhan had been hypnotized before, perhaps many times. While Sirhan was under hypnosis, Dr. Diamond had gotten him to write in a manner that was strangely similar to some of the writing in his notebook, and when he was awakened, Sirhan denied any familiarity with the work that he had just produced. Diamond had also demonstrated that Sirhan was very susceptible to post-hypnotic suggestion. He had Sirhan do things in his normal awake

state that he had been instructed to perform while under hypnosis, with no awareness that he had been programmed.

Not knowing anything about the autopsy or evidence of a second shooter, and taking for granted that there was no conspiracy, Dr. Diamond conjectured that, in Klaber and Melanson's terms, "Sirhan unknowingly programmed himself to murder Robert Kennedy and unknowingly programmed himself to forget his crime — a feat regarded as next to impossible by leading experts in the field of hypnosis."[30]

But other experts in hypnosis and mental manipulation believe that Sirhan has been submitted to hypnotic programming. "It was obvious that he had been programmed to kill Robert Kennedy and programmed to forget that he had been programmed," stated Dr. Robert Blair Kaiser.[31] In 2008, Harvard University professor Daniel Brown, a noted expert in hypnosis and trauma memory loss, interviewed Sirhan for a total of 60 hours. He fist noticed that Sirhan was exceptionably easy to hypnotize, which suggests a previous practice. Brown's extensive tests revealed "actual evidence of hypnotically induced alter personality states." Dr Brown concluded that Sirhan acted involuntarily under the effect of hypnotic suggestion: "His firing of the gun was neither under his voluntary control, nor done with conscious knowledge, but is likely a product of automatic hypnotic behavior and coercive control." During his sessions with Dr. Brown, Sirhan could remember having coffee with an attractive girl, before suddenly finding himself at a shooting range with a weapon he did not know. According to Brown's report, "Mr. Sirhan did not go with the intent to shoot Senator Kennedy, but did respond to a specific hypnotic cue given to him by that woman to enter 'range mode,' during which Mr. Sirhan automatically and involuntarily responded with a 'flashback' that he was shooting at a firing range at circle targets."[32]

In the preceding months, Sirhan had been seen in various gun shooting ranges around Los Angeles, generally accompanied by one or two men. On June 1, he had checked in at Corona Police Department range, accompanied by an unknown instructor, and on June 4, little over 12 hours before shooting at Kennedy, he had signed at the San Gabriel Valley Gun Club, where Everett Buckner, the club's Line Officer on duty throughout the day, heard him talk to a "husky build" blonde woman in her 20s, who answered him "Get away from me, you son of a bitch; they'll recognize you."[33]

With the help of Professor Brown, Sirhan was also able to remember that his instructor had a falling moustache, which fits the description of famous hypnotist William Joseph Bryan Jr. Bryan makes no secret of having worked for the Air Force in the "brainwashing section." His biggest claim to fame was to have exposed, by hypnosis, the Boston Strangler, Albert Di Salvo, who thereafter confessed to the crime. Bryan often bragged about it. This is significant because, among the automatic writings in Sirhan's notebooks, we find this: *"God help me . . . please help me. Salvo Di Di Salvo Die S Salvo."* It is surmised he heard the name while under hypnosis.[34]

We know that in the 1960s, American military agencies were experimenting on mental control. Dr. Sidney Gottlieb, son of Hungarian Jews, directed the infamous CIA MKUltra project, which, among other things, were to answer questions such as: "Can a person under hypnosis be forced to commit murder?" according to a declassified document dated May 1951.[35] It is little known, by the way, that MKUltra was an overwhelmingly Jewish enterprise, with people like Dr. John Gittinger, Harris Isbell, James Keehner, Lauretta Bender, Albert Kligman, Eugene Saenger, Chester Southam, Robert Lashbrook, Harold Abramson, Charles Geschickter, and Ray Treichler.[36]

In his book *Rise and Kill First: The Secret History of Israel's Targeted Assassinations* (2018), Israeli journalist Ronen Bergman has revealed that, in May 1968, the month preceding Robert Kennedy's assassination, the Israeli Military Intelligence (AMAN) was planning to assassinate Yasser Arafat by hypnotically programming a Palestinian. The idea was proposed by a Navy psychologist named Binyamin Shalit, who claimed that, "if he was given a Palestinian prisoner — one of the thousands in Israeli jails — with the right characteristics, he could brainwash and hypnotize him into becoming a programmed killer. He would then be sent across the Jordan, join the Fatah there, and, when the opportunity arose, do away with Arafat." The proposal was approved. Shalit selected a 28-year-old Palestinian from Bethlehem, whom he deemed easily suggestionnable. The operation failed, but it proves that, in 1968 precisely, Israel was practicing a method of assassination identical to the one used against Robert Kennedy.[37]

Moreover, manipulating Palestinians to make them commit crimes, or committing crimes and blaming Palestinians for them, bears the signature of Israel. According to former Mossad agent, Victor Ostrovsky, in 1991 elements of the Mossad were plotting an attempt on the life of President George H. W. Bush. Bush had resisted an unprecedented pro-Israel lobbying campaign that called for $10 billion to help Jews immigrate from the former Soviet Union to Israel, complaining in a televised press conference on September 12 that "one thousand Jewish lobbyists are on Capitol Hill against little old me."[38] Worse, there was his policy of pressuring Israel to the negotiating table at the Madrid Conference by freezing their loan guarantees. Israel had had enough of him. The plan was to leak words to the Spanish police that terrorists were on their way, kill Bush and, in the midst of the confusion, release three Palestinians captured earlier and kill them on the spot.[39]

It is well known that Israel has a long history and a grand expertise in false flag terrorism. A report of the U.S. Army School for Advanced Military Studies (SAMS), quoted by the *Washington Times* on September 10, 2001, described the Israeli Intelligence agency as: "Wildcard. Ruthless and cunning. Has capability to target U.S. forces and make it look like a Palestinian/Arab act."[40] That statement was made public on the day before 9/11.

The pattern dates from before the creation of the Jewish State, with the bombing of the King David Hotel, headquarter of the British authorities in Jerusalem, in the morning of July 22, 1946. Six terrorists of the Irgun dressed as Arabs brought 225 kg of explosives hidden in milk churns into the building. When a British officer became suspicious and gunshot ensued, the Irgun members fled after igniting the explosives. The explosion killed 91 people, mostly British, but also 15 Jews.

The strategy was repeated in Egypt during the summer of 1954, with Operation Susannah. The goal was to compromise the British's withdrawal from the Suez Canal, demanded by Colonel Abdul Gamal Nasser with support from President Eisenhower. Egyptian Jews trained in Israel bombed several British targets, then put the blame on the Muslim Brotherhood. The accidental detonation of an explosive device allowed the exposure of the conspiracy, which led to the "Lavon Affair", from the name of the Defense Minister who was held responsible.

There are more of the same stories in Gordon Thomas's *Gideon's Spies: the Secret History of the Mossad* (2009).[41] By definition, false-flagged Arab terrorism is only exposed when it fails, and we cannot know how many such operations have been set up by the Mossad. But from the revelations of Ronen Bergman in *Rise and Kill First,* Sirhan sure looks like a typical made-in-Mossad Palestinian patsy.

There are still, of course, unanswered questions, such as: How did Sirhan find himself in the kitchen pantry of the Ambassador Hotel at midnight on June 6, 1968, with a pistol in his pocket? Sirhan himself declared it was by accident, or by mistake, but then he doesn't remember much of that evening. Another question is: Why did Kennedy, after finishing his speech, exit the ballroom through the kitchen pantry, instead of walking through the crowd of his supporters, as he usually did? To this question, there is an answer: according to a campaign volunteer present at the scene and interviewed by Michael Piper, it was Robert's Press Secretary Frank Mankiewicz who insisted that Robert go this way.[42] Now, isn't it awkward that Mankiewicz had started his career in public relations "as civil rights director for the western branch of the AntiDefamation League of B'nai B'rith," as he mentions in his autobiography.[43] (The ADL, remember, was founded in 1913 by the B'nai B'rith to defend the convicted child rapist and murderer Leo Frank.)[44] What was a B'nai B'rith member doing around Kennedy? In 1991, Mankiewicz handled publicity for Oliver Stone's film *JFK*.

Was Robert Kennedy really a friend of Israel?

If Sirhan was hypnotically programmed, the question is: Who had some interest in having a visceral anti-Zionist Palestinian blamed for the killing of Robert Kennedy? Israel, of course. But then, we are faced with a dilemma, for why would Israel want to kill Robert Kennedy, if Robert Kennedy was supportive of Israel?

The dilemma rests on a misleading assumption, which is part of the deception. Robert Kennedy was *not* pro-Israel. He was simply campaigning in 1968. As everyone knows, a few good wishes and promises to Israel are an inescapable ritual in such circumstances. Robert's statement in an Oregon synagogue, mentioned in the May 27 Pasadena *Independent Star-News* article found in Sirhan's pocket, didn't exceed the minimal requirements.

Its author David Lawrence had, in another article entitled "Paradoxical Bob," underlined how little credit should be given to such electoral promises: "Presidential candidates are out to get votes and some of them do not realize their own inconsistencies."[45] In fact, as Arthur Krock has noted, the supposed motive for RFK's murder is itself paradoxical: "If this motive was his position that the United States was committed to preserve Israel as a nation, his statement was made with more moderation than that of other important political persons who said the same thing."[46]

All things considered, there is no ground for believing that Robert Kennedy would have been, as president of the U.S.A., particularly Israel-friendly. The Kennedy family was known for its hostility to Jewish influence in politics, and Robert had demonstrated such hostility as Attorney General. He had infuriated Zionist leaders by supporting an investigation led by Senator William Fulbright and the Senate Committee on Foreign Relations, aimed at registering the American Zionist Council as a "foreign agent", which would had considerably hindered its efficiency.[47] We'll come back to it.

Killing Kennedy for being pro-Israel made no sense at all. As a matter of fact, Sirhan cannot remember having ever wanted to kill him. He loved him, like he had loved his brother. During his trial, defense attorney Grant Cooper asked him about his feelings toward President John Kennedy:

"I loved him, sir," Sirhan replied. "More than any American would have." "Why?" "Because just a few weeks before his assassination he was working, sir, with the leaders of the Arab government, the Arab countries, to bring a solution, sir, to the Palestinian refugee problem, and he promised these Arab leaders that he would do his utmost and his best to force or to put some pressure on Israel, sir, to comply with the 1948 United Nations Resolution, sir; to either repatriate those Arab refugees or give them back, give them the right to return to their homes. And when he was killed, sir, that never happened."[48]

In conclusion, it is only with shameless hypocrisy that *The Forward* could write, forty years after Bobby's death: "In remembering Bobby Kennedy, let us remember not just what he lived for, but also what he died for — namely, the precious nature of the American-Israeli relationship."[49] In other words, let us cherish this narrative which is so good for Israel. In 2018 again, for the fiftieth anniversary, the Jewish and Israeli press continues to claim that Robert was killed because he was "pro-Israel".[50]

Of course, the fact that the Zionist media lied and continues to lie when granting Robert Kennedy some posthumous certificate of good will toward Israel, and thereby provides Israel with a fake alibi, is not a sufficient reason for concluding that Israel murdered Robert. Even the fact that the masterminds of the plot chose as their programmed instrument an anti-Zionist Palestinian, and thereby stirred a strong anti-Palestinian feeling among Americans at the same time as getting rid of Robert, does not prove that Israel was involved. Nor does, of course, the fact that Samuel Yorty, the Jewish mayor of Los Angeles (home to the nation's second largest Jewish community after New York, gangsters included) was extremely active spreading the narrative of a "crime against Israel"[51] What is still lacking for a serious presumption is a plausible motive.

The motive of Robert's assassination must be found, not in what Robert publicly declared in a synagogue during his presidential campaign, but rather in what he confided only to his closest friends: his intention to reopen the investigation on his brother's death.

Our next question, therefore, is: What would a real investigation, conducted under the supervision of Robert in the White House, have revealed?

CHAPTER 2
JFK and the Samson Option

The "CIA-did-it" theory

It is obvious to anybody just vaguely informed that a genuine investigation into John Kennedy's assassination would first establish that Oswald was a mere "patsy", as he said himself, a scapegoat prepared in advance to be blamed for the crime and then disposed of. I will not here review the evidence that contradicts the official thesis of the lone gunner. It is well known and can be found in numerous books and documentary films.

Just as notorious is the theory that the plot to kill Kennedy originated from a secret network within the CIA, in collusion with extremist elements in the Pentagon. In general, as Tim Tate and Brad Johnson write:

> The Central Intelligence Agency features so routinely in stories of alleged conspiracies that it has become essentially the Ur-conspiracy: an ill-motivated, all-encompassing explanation for the majority of unexplained, or contested, causes célèbres since the end of the Second World War. Hollywood movies and television dramas feed this trope, re-enforcing public suspicion and with it the claims of those who promote claims of secret Agency machinations.[52]

The "CIA-killed-JFK" conspiracy theory looms the largest in books, articles and films that have been produced since John Kennedy died. In fact, mainstream newspapers and publishing houses have played some role in steering conspiracy-minded people toward the CIA trail. One major contributor was Mark Lane (born Levin) in a 1966 book, *Rush to Judgment*, which received considerable media coverage. Lane was even more adamant that the CIA was the culprit in his last book, published in 2011: *Last Word: My Indictment of the CIA in the Murder of JFK.*

Another contributor to the same effort was the Israeli-American Alan Weberman, with his 1975 book *Coup d'État in America: The CIA and the Assassination of John F. Kennedy,* for which he acknowledged Richard Perle's assistance. According to the Jewish daily *Forward* (December 28, 2012), Weberman had "immigrated to Israel in 1959 and has dual American-Israeli citizenship," and is "a close associate of Jewish Defense Organization founder Mordechai Levy, whose fringe group is a spin-off of the late Rabbi Meir Kahane's militant right-wing Jewish Defense League."[53]

That Israeli agents in various spheres of power have been instrumental in spreading conspiracy theories targeting the CIA is also evidenced by Oliver Stone's film *JFK* released in 1991, starring Kevin Costner as Jim Garrison. This film, which shook public opinion to the point of motivating the *President John F. Kennedy Assassination Records Collection Act* of 1992, was produced by Arnon Milchan, described in a 2011 biography as "one of the most important covert agents that Israeli intelligence has ever fielded," involved from his youth in arms smuggling from the U.S. to Israel.[54] In 2013 Milchan publicly revealed his extended activity as a secret Israeli agent, working specially to boost Israel's nuclear program.[55] It is therefore no wonder that Stone's scenario, co-written by Zachary Sklar, makes no allusion to the Mossad connection that Garrison had stumbled upon.

I will come back to the CIA's role in JFK's assassination in chapter 5. In this and the three following chapters, I am going to argue that the Israeli leadership was the prime mover in the Kennedy assassination. And by "the Israeli leadership," I mean primarily David Ben-Gurion, who served as Prime Minister and Defense Minister from 1948 to 1963, with one brief interlude. Let's start with the motives.

THE TIMES OF ISRAEL

Hollywood producer Arnon Milchan reveals past as secret agent

Filmmaker, long rumored to be a real-life James Bond, talks about how he helped Israel's alleged nuclear-bomb program

By STUART WINER ⌄
25 November 2013, 12:20 am | ⵊⵊ 10

      258 shares

Kennedy, Israel and the Arab world

Kennedy felt no sympathy for Israel's anachronistic colonial adventure, but great admiration for Abdul Gamal Nasser, the hero of Arab nationalism. Historian Philip Muehlenbeck writes: "While the Eisenhower administration had sought to isolate Nasser and reduce his influence through building up Saudi Arabia's King Saud as a conservative rival to the Egyptian president, the Kennedy administration pursued the exact opposite strategy." Kennedy appointed John Badeau, a scholar with a deep knowledge of Arabic language and culture, as ambassador to Cairo, and he named Robert Komer, an advocate of closer U.S. ties with Nasser, in the National Security Council with the portfolio of Middle Eastern affairs.[56]

During his first months in the White House, Kennedy committed himself by letters to Nasser and other Arab heads of State to support U.N. Resolution 194 for the right of return of Palestinian refugees. Ben-Gurion reacted with a letter to the Israeli ambassador in Washington, intended to be circulated among Jewish American leaders, in which he stated: "Israel will regard this plan as a more serious danger to her existence than all the threats of the Arab dictators and kings, than all the Arab armies, than all of Nasser's missiles and his Soviet MIGs. . . . Israel will fight against this implementation down to the last man."[57]

On November 20, 1963, two days before President Kennedy's death, his delegation to the United Nations was, again, urging Israel to implement Resolution 194. Kennedy never read the outraged reactions in the *London Jewish Chronicle* of November 22: "Prime Minister Levi Eshkol summoned the U.S. ambassador . . . and told him that Israel was 'shocked' by the pro-Arab attitude adopted by the U.S. delegation." Golda Meir, for her part, "expressed Israel's 'astonishment and anger' at the attitude of the U.S."[58]

Kennedy was mourned in the Arab world, where his portrait graced many homes. Under Johnson, American foreign policy was reversed again, without the American people being aware of it. Johnson cut the economic aid to Egypt and boosted the aid to Israel, which reached $92 million in 1966, more than 70 percent of which financed military equipment.[59] Conversely, by denying Egypt and Algeria U.S. aid, Johnson forced them to turn to the Soviet Union in their effort to keep up with Israel's militarization.

Another thorn in Israel's side was the Kennedys' determination to reduce the influence of the euphemistically called "Israel Lobby". During his 1960 presidential campaign, Kennedy had been approached by Zionist financier Abraham Feinberg, whose business, writes Seymour Hersh, was "to ensure continued Democratic Party support for Israel." Here is how Kennedy summed up Feinberg's message, to his friend Charles Bartlett: "We know your campaign is in trouble. We're willing to pay your bills if you'll let us have control of your Middle East policy." Bartlett recalls that Kennedy was deeply upset and decided that, "if he ever did get to be President, he was going to do something about it."[60]

In the meantime, though, Kennedy had to yield to some extent. For the position of Secretary of State, his first choice was William Fulbright, who was the chairman of the Senate Committee on Foreign Relations. Arthur Schlesinger Jr. wrote in his diary that Jewish pressure "killed Fulbright", and the post was given to Dean Rusk, a more consensual character who turned out to be rather ineffective.[61] Rusk, in turn, opposed some of Kennedy's choices for ambassadors, and chose for Vietnam the Republican Henry Cabot Lodge, a longtime Boston enemy of the Kennedys who sabotaged Kennedy's policy.[62]

Senator Fulbright, however, took his revenge. The Committee on Foreign Relations conducted an audit regarding "an increasing number of incidents involving attempts by foreign governments, or their agents, to influence the conduct of American foreign policy by techniques outside normal diplomatic channels." The Committee concluded that by virtue of its funding coming in through the State of Israel, the American Zionist Council must be registered as a "foreign agent" and therefore subject to the obligations defined by the Foreign Agents Registration Act of 1938. [63] That would have considerably hindered its corrupting influence. After months of back and forth, on October 11, 1963 the New York law firm representing the AZC received a formal written demand from Attorney General RFK's office to immediately (within 72 hours) proceed to register as a foreign agent. Forms for said registration accompanied the letter.

After the assassination of John Kennedy, Rusk served Johnson till the end. Nicholas Katzenbach took over the position of Robert Kennedy as Attorney General and buried the procedure against the AZC. The AZC's lobbying division, the American Israel Public Affairs Committee (AIPAC), became the most powerful special interest group in American political life. In 1973, Fulbright could say: "Israel controls the U.S. Senate. . . . The great majority of the Senate of the U.S. — somewhere around 80 percent — are completely in support of Israel; anything Israel wants, Israel gets."[64]

Dimona's ticking bomb

The most plausible motive for Israel to kill John Kennedy has been revealed by Seymour Hersh in *The Samson Option* in 1991, and in a more academic style by Avner Cohen in *Israel and the Bomb* in 1998, and the lead has been followed up in 2007 by Michael Karpin in *The Bomb in the Basement.* What these investigators reveal is that Kennedy, informed by the CIA in 1960 of the military aim pursued at the Dimona complex in the Negev desert, was firmly determined to force Israel to renounce it. With that purpose in mind, he replaced CIA Director Allen Dulles by

John McCone, who had, as Eisenhower's chairman of the Atomic Energy Commission (AEC), leaked to *The New York Times* the truth about Israel's Dimona project; the story was printed on December 19, 1960, weeks before Kennedy was to take office. As Alan Hart writes, "there can be no doubt that Kennedy's determination to stop Israel developing its own nuclear bomb was the prime factor in his decision to appoint McCone."[65]

Kennedy had made global nuclear disarmament his historical mission. He understood that nuclear weapons are the negation of all historical efforts to restrain war and spare civilians. This abomination had to be eradicated. On September 25, 1961, after less than a year in power, he declared before the United Nations' General Assembly:

> Today, every inhabitant of this planet must contemplate the day when this planet may no longer be habitable. Every man, woman and child lives under a nuclear sword of Damocles, hanging by the slenderest of threads, capable of being cut at any moment by accident or miscalculation or by madness. The weapons of war must be abolished before they abolish us. . . . It is therefore our intention to challenge the Soviet Union, not to an arms race, but to a peace race — to advance together step by step, stage by stage, until general and complete disarmament has been achieved.

The program Kennedy outlined "would achieve under the eyes of an international disarmament organization, a steady reduction in force, both nuclear and conventional, until it has abolished all armies and all weapons except those needed for internal order and a new United Nations Peace Force."[66] It was the speech that would inspire Khrushchev's first private letter to Kennedy — a letter of 26 pages.

Early in 1963, Kennedy vigorously engaged his country in the direction of disarmament. May 6, he addressed directive NSAM-239 entitled "U.S. Disarmament Proposals" to all government administrations, both military and civilian, inviting them to cooperate with the Arms Control and Disarmament Agency created in 1961, by making proposals towards the goal of "general and complete disarmament." This phrase is repeated in his famous "Peace Speech" of June 10, delivered at the American University of Washington before a crowd of students: "Our primary long-range interest is general and complete disarmament — designed to take place by stages, permitting parallel political developments to build the new institutions of peace which would take the place of arms." In that speech, Kennedy made public his negotiations with Khrushchev towards global disarmament, which would lead, as a first step, to the first treaty limiting nuclear testing.

To have his Test Ban Treaty accepted by a reluctant Congress, he launched an ambitious communication campaign and spoke directly to the nation on television on July 26, 1963, building the people's awareness of the urgency of stopping an arm race that could lead to "a full-scale nuclear exchange" after which "the living would envy the dead."[67] The treaty, which prohibited nuclear testing in the atmosphere and under water, was signed in August 1963 by the Soviet Union, the United States and the United Kingdom. "No other single accomplishment in the White House ever gave Kennedy greater satisfaction," according to Ted Sorensen, who helped craft the treaty.[68] Six weeks later, on September 20, Kennedy expressed his pride and hope before the United Nations' Assembly, calling his Test Ban Treaty a first "lever" by which to "move the world" (Archimedes): "My fellow inhabitants of this planet, let us take our stand here in this Assembly of nations. And let us see if we, in our own time, can move the world to a just and lasting peace."[69]

In the sixties, nuclear disarmament was an achievable goal, since only four or five countries had nuclear weapons. There was a historic opportunity, and Kennedy was determined not to let it pass. "I am haunted by the feeling that by 1970, unless we are successful, there may be ten nuclear powers instead of four, and by 1975, fifteen or twenty," he said prophetically during a press conference on March 21, 1963.[70] Following the impetus of the two imperial powers, all countries would cooperate towards nuclear disarmament.

All countries but one. In the early 1950s, David Ben-Gurion, both Prime Minister and Defense Minister, entrusted Shimon Peres to start the secret manufacture of atomic bombs by using fuel provided by France and by diverting from its pacific aim the cooperation program Atoms for Peace, launched naively by Eisenhower. Avner Cohen explains in *Israel and the Bomb* that David Ben-Gurion was firmly convinced that without nuclear bombs Israel would not survive. "Ben Gurion was consumed by fears for Israel's security," and "over the years Ben Gurion's fears and anxieties became national policy." Ben-Gurion's determination to make Israel a nuclear state "stemmed from his understanding of the geopolitical realities of the Arab-Israeli

conflict." He believed that the Arabs would never accept the losses
of the 1948 war unless they were persuaded that any attempt to
regain them was futile. Therefore, "The only solution to Israel's
security problem was a robust deterrent force."[71]

Avner Cohen added, in an interview with Jefferson Morley: "In
the eyes of the Israelis, there was no undertaking that was more
important, more secretive, more costly, more existential — more
sacred — than the nuclear project. Everything is kosher, everything is okay, in order to make it happen. *Everything*. It was almost
like a religious commitment to make it happen: The bomb is a way
to ensure survival after the Holocaust."[72] (Preventing Iran from
getting the bomb is now of the same order of importance: between
2007 and 2012, at least six Iranian nuclear scientists have been
murdered by Mossad.[73])

Kennedy had been informed by Eisenhower before taking
office that Ben-Gurion's assurance that the Israeli complex in the
Negev desert was "designed exclusively for peaceful purposes"
(Ben-Gurion's statement at the Knesset on December 21, 1960)
was not to be trusted. He asked his Secretary of State Dean Rusk to
investigate and keep him informed. Two AEC scientists were
allowed to visit Dimona on May 17, 1961, but the large
underground reprocessing plant under construction was kept
hidden from them. They reported in their two-page memo that they
saw "no present evidence that the Israelis have weapons
production in mind". "Israel could not have hoped for a better
report," comments Avner Cohen. "It is striking how uncritically
the American technical experts accepted what the Israelis had told
them about the project."[74]

On May 30, Kennedy met Ben-Gurion at the Waldorf Astoria
Hotel in New York. It is worth quoting extensively the memorandum of that meeting, since it gives a good sense of the nature of
the dialogue between the two heads of state. It begins like this:
"After an exchange of amenities . . . the President and Prime
Minister Ben Gurion plunged into a discussion of Israel's Dimona
reactor." Kennedy expressed satisfaction about the May 17 visit,
and added, very diplomatically: "our problem is how to dissemi-
nate information about the nature of the reactor in a such a way as
to remove any doubts other nations might have as to Israel's
peaceful purposes." Ben-Gurion then brazenly lied to him, either
taking him for an idiot or asking him to pretend he is one: "The
Prime Minister said he wanted to talk about the reactor in the

context of Israel's problems. The greatest of these problems, and an almost insoluble one, he described as Israel's serious shortage of fresh water. . . . Israel hopes that atomic power . . . will make possible the economic desalinization of sea water. . . . Israel's main — and for the time being, only — purpose is this, the Prime Minister said." Kennedy politely ignored the lie and came back to his point, asking Ben-Gurion "to let neutral scientists also observe the reactor." Ben-Gurion agreed to the principle, but "then raised the question of Israel's security" pointing at the military strength of the United Arab Republic. "'If they should defeat us, they would do to the Jews what Hitler did.' He asserted also that the Arabs do not value human life and that this makes the problem more difficult." Ben-Gurion said that Eisenhower had promised him Hawks missiles, but Kennedy answered that he "had not found records" of such promise, and that, "while the Hawk is a defensive weapon it is also a missile and should missile come into the Middle Eastern area, military weaponry will escalate fast."[75]

It was not before September 1962 that Kennedy and his CIA director John McCone overcame Ben-Gurion's opposition for a new inspection. Here is how Seymour Hersh describes the way the Israelis prepared for it, highlighting Abraham Feinberg's role in the deception:

> a false control room was constructed at Dimona, complete with false control panels and computer-driven measuring devices . . . The goal was to convince the inspectors that no chemical reprocessing plant existed or was possible. One big fear was that the Americans would seek to inspect the reactor core physically . . . It was agreed that the inspection team would not be permitted to enter the core "for safety reasons." In Abe Feinberg's view, Kennedy's unyielding demand for an inspection had left Israel with no option: "It was part of my job to tip them off that Kennedy was insisting on this. So they gave him a scam job."[76]

But, Hersh notes, "The President was far too politically astute not to understand, as he angrily told his friend Charles Bartlett, that the Israeli 'sons of bitches lie to me constantly about their nuclear capability.'"[77]

Soon after, the Cuban missile crisis that had almost triggered a nuclear confrontation with the USSR put the Dimona problem back on Kennedy's top priorities. In the beginning of 1963, reports indicated that Israel was most likely progressing toward a nuclear-weapons option. On 2 April, Kennedy presented Ben-Gurion his request for semiannual U.S. visits to Dimona, beginning in May. Ben-Gurion stalled, then on 25 April, protested to Kennedy with a seven-page letter arguing that a recent Arab proclamation to "liberate Palestine" was tantamount to planning a new holocaust, since "the 'liberation of Palestine' is impossible without the total destruction of the people of Israel." He pleaded again, on May 12: "Mr. President, my people have the right to exist ... and this existence is in danger."[78]

Kennedy would not budge, and on May 17 insisted again on "periodic visits to Dimona," arguing: "it is difficult to imagine that the Arabs would refrain from turning to the Soviet Union for assistance if Israel were to develop a nuclear weapons capability, what with all the consequences this would hold." Ten days later, Ben-Gurion formally accepted the principle of Kennedy's request, but refused to commit himself on the details.[79]

On 15 June 1963, Kennedy issued a blunt ultimatum letter to Ben-Gurion, requiring a first visit "early this summer" as a condition, he said, for "resolving all doubts as to the peaceful nature intent of the Dimona project," and stating that American commitment to Israel could be "seriously jeopardized" in case of refusal.[80] The very next day, Ben-Gurion stunned Israel and the world by suddenly and unexpectedly resigning for "personal reasons", thereby avoiding receiving Kennedy's letter.

Had he plunged into the underworld of deep politics, where assassinations are plotted? We know at least that he had not given up on Israel's vital need for the nuclear option. Eleven days after resigning from office, he declared, in a farewell address to the employees of the Armaments Development Authority (RAFAEL):

> I do not know of any other nation whose neighbors declare that they wish to terminate it, and not only declare, but prepare for it by all means available to them. We must have no illusions that what is declared every day in Cairo, Damascus, and Iraq are just words. This is the thought that guides the Arab leaders. . . . Our numbers are small, and there is no chance that we could compare ourselves with America's 180 million, or with any Arab neighboring state. There is one thing, however, in which we are not inferior to any other people in the world — this is the Jewish brain. And the Jewish brain does not disappoint; Jewish science does not disappoint. . . . I am confident . . . that science is able to provide us with the weapons that will serve the peace and deter our enemies.[81]

As soon as the new Prime Minister Levi Eshkol took office, Kennedy wrote to him (July 4) in terms similar to those he had used with Ben-Gurion:

> As I wrote to Mr. Ben Gurion, this government's commitment to and support of Israel could be seriously jeopardized if it should be thought that we were unable to obtain reliable information on a subject as vital to peace as the question of Israel's effort in the nuclear field. . . . If Israel's purposes are to be clear beyond reasonable doubt, I believe that the schedule which would best serve our common purposes would be a visit early this summer, another visit in June 1964, and thereafter at intervals of six months. . . . It would be essential . . . that our scientists have access to all areas of the Dimona site and to any related part of the complex, such as fuel fabrication facilities or plutonium separation plant, and that sufficient time be allotted for a thorough examination.[82]

Eshkol tried to gain time by making unsatisfactory proposals of one yearly visit, which was not sufficient to verify the reactor's real purposes. On 19 August, Eshkol came up with a vague response agreeing to a first visit at the end of 1963. By that time, the Dimona reactor would have gone critical, and Kennedy would have realized that he had been fooled.

Meanwhile, some people were busy making sure that Kennedy would be dead by then, with the foreknowledge that Johnson, who owed his career to Abraham Feinberg, would bury the whole affair. Under Johnson, Israel's military nuclear program could proceed as planned, under U.S. tacit protection. U.S. diplomats did make a basic visit to Dimona in January 1964 and reported that, although "the Dimona reactor went critical on December 26, 1963," they found no "weapons-related activities" and left with the impression "that research was the present intention of the Israelis with the Dimona reactor."[83]

It is clear that JFK's assassination solved an intense crisis over Israel's secret nuclear program. A *Haaretz* review of Avner Cohen's book puts it this way: "The murder of American President John F. Kennedy brought to an abrupt end the massive pressure being applied by the US administration on the government of Israel to discontinue the nuclear program. Cohen demonstrates at length the pressures applied by Kennedy on Ben-Gurion. . . . The book implied that, had Kennedy remained alive, it is doubtful whether Israel would today have a nuclear option."[84]

Missing links

For 50 years, the case against Israel in the Kennedy assassination has been smothered, and anyone who mentioned it was quickly ostracized. One single author has seriously followed that lead: Michael Collins Piper, in his 1995 book *Final Judgment.* He was largely ignored by the mainstream of the Kennedy truth movement. But his work has carved its own path nevertheless. In 2013, Martin Sandler mentioned Piper's theory in his edition of letters by Kennedy, which included those addressed to Ben-Gurion about Dimona: "Of all the conspiracy theories," Sandler said, "it remains one of the most intriguing." It is, in fact, a theory widely held in Arab countries. Libyan leader Muammar Gaddafi once declared publicly:

> Kennedy decided to monitor the Dimona nuclear plant. He insisted on doing so, in order to determine whether or not it produces nuclear weapons. The Israelis refused, but he insisted. This crisis was resolved with the resignation of Ben Gurion. He resigned so he would not have to agree to the monitoring of the Dimona plant, and he gave the green light for the killing of Kennedy. Kennedy was killed because he insisted on the monitoring of the Dimona plant.[85]

On September 23, 2009, Gaddafi had the guts to demand a new investigation on Kennedy in front of the U.N. General Assembly. Two years later, he was brutally murdered and his country ravaged by civil war.[86]

That Ben-Gurion ordered the killing of President Kennedy is a theory entertained by many informed Israelis and American Jews. I take as a sure sign of this a column published by Andrew Adler, owner and editor in chief of *The Atlanta Jewish Times,* in January 13, 2012. Unhappy with President Obama's softness on Iran and his "belief that diplomacy is the answer," Adler suggested to the Israeli Prime Minister Benyamin Netanyahu that he "give the go-ahead for U.S.-based Mossad agents to take out a president deemed unfriendly to Israel in order for the current Vice-President to take his place and forcefully dictate that the United States' policy includes its helping the Jewish State obliterate its enemies." Adler assumes that the option "has been discussed in Israel's most inner circle."[87] Where can such an idea come from, except from the assumption that the method has been used successfully in the past?

In this chapter, we have found a plausible motive for Israel to eliminate Kennedy. What remains to be done is to find evidence that the Israeli deep state and its *sayanim* on American soil had the means and the opportunity.

JFK's trip to Dallas (the city with the largest Jewish community in Texas) was sponsored by a powerful business group known as the Dallas Citizens Council, dominated by Julius Schepps, "a wholesale liquor distributor, member of every synagogue in town, and de facto leader of the Jewish community," as described by Bryan Edward Stone in *The Chosen Folks: Jews on the Frontiers of Texas.*[88] Kennedy was on his way to the reception organized in his honor when he was shot.

The Dallas Citizens Council may have been intimately connected to the local B'nai B'rith. Another notorious member was Abraham Zapruder, the man who filmed the assassination and sold his film for $150,000 to *Life magazine*. Zapruder was a garment manufacturer headquartered in the Dallas-Textiles Building (or Dal-Tex).

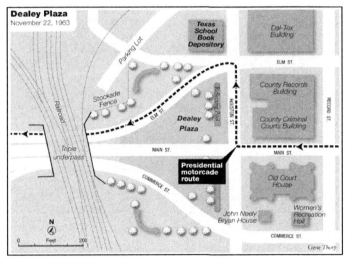

According to the best ballistic studies, it was from this building, and not from the Texas School Book Depository where Oswald was working, that the first shots were fired in Dealey Plaza. They missed, which is why the secondary team, positioned behind the stockade fence on the "grassy knoll", entered into

action and fired the fatal bullet.[89] The Dal-Tex Building was a
hotbed of the Jewish business community in Dallas. It was owned
by David Weisblat, an Anti-Defamation League financier, and Morris
Douglas Jaffe, a Texas oilman described as "a friend and contributor
of President Lyndon B. Johnson" by the *New York Times.*[90]

The "host committee" inviting Kennedy was chaired by
another influential figure of the Jewish community in Dallas:
advertising executive Sam Bloom. According to former British
intelligence officer Colonel John Hughes-Wilson, it was Bloom
who, after Oswald's arrest, suggested to the Police "that they move
the alleged assassin from the Dallas police station to the Dallas
County Jail in order to give the newsmen a good story and
pictures." Oswald was shot by Jack Ruby during that transfer, and
"when the police later searched Ruby's home, they found a slip of
paper with Bloom's name, address and telephone number on it."[91]

We'll talk about Jack Ruby in chapter 4. Before that, we need
to scrutinize the most obvious suspect, the single man who profited
most from the assassination of his president: Lyndon Johnson.
After all, JFK's trip to Dallas had been his idea in the first place.
As a former Texas senator, he had all the accomplices he needed
there to prepare the ambush and make sure the Dallas police would
raise no objection afterwards to the lone gunner theory.

As soon as President Kennedy was declared dead, Johnson
insisted to be sworn in, and managed to drag a traumatized Jackie
by his side, for a picture that was printed in almost every national
and local newspaper the following day, to reassure Americans
about Johnson's legitimacy.

Johnson then set up the Warren Commission, with the task of confirming the conclusion that his friend Edgar Hoover had already released — and no one could contradict Hoover. Apart from its chairman Earl Warren, chosen for his figurative role as Chief Justice, all key people in the investigative Commission were either personal enemies of Kennedy — like Allen Dulles — or ardent Zionists. The man who played the key role in fabricating the government lie purveyed by the Warren Commission was Arlen Specter, the inventor of what came to be known as the "magic bullet" theory: a single bullet supposed to have caused seven wounds to Kennedy and John Connally in the limousine, and later found in pristine condition on a gurney in Parkland Memorial Hospital in Dallas. Specter was the son of Russian Jewish immigrants, and, at his death in 2012, he was honored by the Israeli government as "an unswerving defender of the Jewish State," and by AIPAC, as "a leading architect of the congressional bond between our country and Israel."[92]

CHAPTER 3
LBJ, Israel's Best Friend

Israel had three plausible motives to kill John Kennedy. They are, by order of importance and urgency:

- Dimona: Kennedy, who had made nuclear disarmament his grand mission on the international level, and had taken steps with Khrushchev, was determined to prevent Israel from becoming another nuclear state. For Ben-Gurion, this was a threat to Israel's very survival.

- Nasser: Kennedy had reversed Eisenhower's foreign policy in a pro-Nasser direction, and committed the U.S. to support U.N. Resolution 194 for the right of return of Palestinian refugees, another direct attack at the very identity of the Jewish State.

- AIPAC: Disturbed by Israel's undue influence on American foreign policy, John and Robert Kennedy were determined to curtail, for a start, the American Zionist Council by forcing it to register as a "foreign agent". Ben-Gurion knew that Israel's survival depended on U.S. support, which itself depended on Israel's capacity to maneuver U.S. foreign policy through Jewish organizations in the U.S.

These were powerful motives to get rid of Kennedy, but only with the assurance that the new occupant of the White House would reverse these policies. We should not lose sight of the self-evident truth that the purpose of the Dallas coup was to put Johnson in power.

Johnson did not disappoint. First, thanks to him, Israel could carry on its military nuclear program undisturbed, and acquire its first atomic bomb sometime between 1965 and 1967. Historian Stephen Green says it bluntly in *Taking Sides: America's Secret Relations with a Militant Israel*:

> Perhaps the most significant development of 1963 for the Israeli nuclear weapons program, however, occurred on November 22: on a plane flying from Dallas to Washington, D.C., Lyndon Johnson was sworn in as the 36th President of the United States, following the assassination of John F. Kennedy.... In the early years of the Johnson administration the Israeli nuclear weapons program was referred to in Washington as "the delicate topic." Lyndon Johnson's White House saw no Dimona, heard no Dimona, and spoke no Dimona when the reactor went critical in early 1964.[93]

Faced with Johnson's complete lack of interest for that issue, John McCone resigned from the CIA in 1965, declaring: "When I cannot get the President to read my reports, then it's time to go." As Avner Cohen and William Burr put it in a recent *Haaretz* article, with Johnson looking the other way, "Israel built a nuclear program right under the Americans' nose."[94] It was not until 1986 that the world realized it, with the publication in the *Sunday Times* of photographs taken inside the Dimona Complex by Israeli technician Mordechai Vanunu. This triggered an inevitable nuclear arms race that now makes Israel itself more paranoid, blaming Iran for a program that they themselves developed clandestinely and continue to deny.

Secondly, at the Department of Justice, Johnson replaced Robert Kennedy by Nicholas Katzenbach, who buried the proce-dure for registering the American Zionist Council as a "foreign agent". (Katzenbach was also instrumental in the formation of the Warren Commission, and would later be moved to the State Department in anticipation of the Six Day War.)

Thirdly, Johnson cut economic aid to Egypt and boosted military aid to Israel. He lifted the embargo on offensive military equipment, and U.S.-made tanks and aircrafts flowed to Tel Aviv.

According to Stephen Green, "The $92 million in military assistance provided in fiscal year 1966 was greater than the total of all official military aid provided to Israel cumulatively in all the years going back to the foundation of that nation in 1948."[95] No wonder the coming to power of Johnson was greeted with relief in the Israeli press. With Johnson's help, Israel would defeat in six days her most formidable enemy, vastly superior in size and population. She would more than double her territory in violation of international law, and suffer no penalty.

⊗HAARETZ Sunday, May 16, 2021. Sivan 5, 5781 Time in Israel: 4:09 PM

Israel News | All sections | Biblical 'toilet' | Tucker - Israel | James Packer | COVID | What to watch for

Home > U.S. News

Lyndon Johnson: Israel Has Had No Better Friend

Historians generally regard Johnson as the president most uniformly friendly to Israel

JTA and Ron Kampeas | May 09, 2016 5:14 PM

American voters were kept unaware of this 180-degree turn in U.S. foreign policy. But today, as we are told in an article from the *Jewish Telegraphic Agency* taken up by *Haaretz,* "Historians generally regard Johnson as the president most uniformly friendly to Israel":

> Johnson was the first president to invite an Israeli prime minister, Levi Eshkol, on a state visit. . . . LBJ soon abandoned pressure on Israel to come clean about the Dimona reactor. He increased arms sales to Israel and in 1968, after Israel's primary supplier, France, imposed an embargo as a means of cultivating ties in the Arab world, the United States became Israel's main supplier of weapons, notably launching the talks that would lead to the sale of Phantom fighter jets to Israel. . . . during the [1967 Six-Day] war, he ordered warships to within 50 miles of Syria's coast as a

warning to the Soviets not to interfere. In a speech in the war's immediate aftermath, Johnson effectively nipped in the bud any speculation that the United States would pressure Israel to unilaterally give up the lands it had captured. He laid down not only the "land for peace" formula that would inform subsequent U.N. Security Council resolutions, but made it clear that any formula had to ensure Jewish access to Jerusalem's Old City.[96]

Johnson's high treason for Israel

In 1956, the U.S.A. under Eisenhower had opposed the invasion of the Suez Canal by Israel. Kennedy pursued the same policy of restraining Israel's expansionism. In contrast, in June 1967, Johnson would give Israel a green light for its "preemptive" war against Egypt.[97] In a letter dated June 3, Johnson assured Israeli Prime Minister Levi Eshkol: "I want to protect the territorial integrity of Israel . . . and will provide as effective American support as possible to preserve the peace and freedom of your nation and of the area."[98] Two days earlier, in a Washington meeting on May 30, the CIA provided Mossad chief Meir Amit photos taken from satellites and spy planes, which enabled Israel to precisely locate the Egyptian airfields and destroy its air force within six days.

Four days after the start of the Israeli attack, Nasser accepted the ceasefire request from the U.N. Security Council. It was too early for the Israelis, who had not yet achieved all their territorial objectives. Johnson withheld any effort toward a ceasefire, and ordered the State Department to back away from their previous statement that "Our position is neutral in thought, word and deed."[99]

Then, on June 8, the USS *Liberty*, an unarmed NSA spy ship flying a large American flag, stationed in international waters off Sinai, after having been flown over and photographed all morning by Israeli planes, was suddenly attacked by several unmarked Mirage jets, as well as Mystère fighter-bombers dropping napalm, and torpedoed by three Israeli-flagged PT boats. Based on the numerous testimonies from survivors, who spoke again in front of cameras for the film *Sacrificing Liberty* (2021), directed by Matthew Skow, the obvious intent of the attackers was, after having first destroyed all antennas on the ship, to sink her and leave no survivors: even stretcher bearers and life rafts were machine-gunned.

The attack would have been blamed on Egypt if it had succeeded. It would then have given Johnson a pretext for intervening on the side of Israel against Egypt, rallying American public support under the perfect-sounding battle cry "Remember the Liberty!"[100] Soon after the attack, aircrafts possibly loaded with nuclear bombs were actually launched from the USS *America* stationed in the Mediterranean, and the U.S. Embassy in Cairo warned of an imminent bombing on the city. Egypt being allied to the Soviets, the conflict might have escalated into a world war.

But the false-flag operation failed. First, just after the initial attack by unmarked aircrafts, the crew managed to send an SOS, which was picked up by the aircraft carrier USS *Saratoga*, stationed 500 miles away with the Sixth Fleet. Captain Joseph Tully, commanding officer of the *Saratoga,* immediately launched 12 aircrafts conventionally armed to rescue the USS *Liberty*. Almost immediately, a message came to Tully from Rear Admiral Lawrence Geis to return all aircrafts to their carriers. Geis would later tell having himself received that order from Defense Secretary McNamara on the phone. When Geis challenged the order, LBJ grabbed the telephone and said firmly: "Recall the damned aircrafts. I don't care if the ship sinks and all the sailors are killed, I will not embarrass my ally." That was before anyone had been notified that the attackers were Israelis.[101]

By some miracle, the Israelis torpedoes failed to sink the ship. After 75 minutes of strafing, bombing and torpedoing, the Israelis gave up, possibly because of the approach of a Soviet ship. Orders then came from the White House to call back the U.S. aircrafts on their way to bomb Cairo. They were seven minutes from target when Admiral William Inman Martin recalled them.[102] 17 hours later, rescue came at last for the USS *Liberty*. More than 200 men, mostly engineers, technicians and translators, were dead or seriously wounded.

After Israel admitted being the aggressor, pretending to have mistaken the USS *Liberty* for an Egyptian warship, Johnson sent his National Security Advisor Walt Rostow to tell the Chairman of the Joint Chiefs and the Secretary of the Navy to forget about the incident. "I could never imagine," Rostow sententiously declared, "any Israeli, no matter what his politics were, deliberately firing on the American flag."[103] The affair was suppressed by a court of inquiry headed by Admiral John Sidney McCain Sr., Commander-in-Chief of U.S. Naval Forces in Europe (and father of future presidential candidate Senator John McCain III). Its report was a complete travesty, not including any of the key Israel-incriminating testimony by officers and crew of the *Liberty*. The official story was a case of "mistaken identity" and "targeting error". The survivors received a medal in an unadvertised ceremony, accompanied by a formal order never to mention the incident, under the threat of the most severe reprisal. Johnson made no reproach to Israel. Rather, six months later, he invited Israeli Prime Minister Levi Eshkol to Washington. "They got along so well — both men were farmers — that Johnson paid Eshkol the rare compliment of inviting him to his ranch," writes Ron Kampeas.[104]

Like Israel's secret fabrication of nuclear bombs, the story of the USS *Liberty* only became known in the 1990s, when some of the survivors broke the silence. In 2014 Al-Jazeera produced the documentary *The Day Israel Attacked America,* and in 2021 was released the groundbreaking four-part documentary film *Sacrificing Liberty* (2021), including extensive testimonies from survivors and other people involved.[105]

Israel learned the lesson. In *The Passionate Attachment,* former Undersecretary of State George Ball wrote: "by permitting a cover-up of Israel's attack on the Liberty, President Johnson told the Israelis in effect that nothing they did would induce American politicians to refuse their bidding. From that time forth, the Israelis began to act as if they had an inalienable right to American aid and backing."[106]

But it is clear, from Admiral Geis's testimony, that Johnson didn't just cover Israel after the fact; he had secretly authorized Israel's war crime and treachery. According to Peter Hounam, author of *Operation Cyanide: Why the Bombing of the USS Liberty Nearly Caused World War III* (2003), and contributor to the film *Sacrificing Liberty* (episode IV), the attack on the *Liberty* had been authorized by the White House as part of "a secret political agreement in 1966 by which Israel and the U.S. had vowed to destroy Nasser."[107]

Nor is it correct to infer, as Stephen Green does, that "by June of 1967 ... Lyndon Johnson and his team of foreign-policy advisors had completely revised U.S.-Israeli relations. To all intents and purposes, Israel had become the 51st state." Calling Israel the 51st state is a euphemism: what changed under Johnson is not that the U.S. started protecting Israel as if it were of part of the

United States, but that Israel took control of U.S. foreign policy with no regard for U.S. interests. Israel's influence on the U.S. is best described as that of a parasite,[108] and this illustrated by the Israeli presence in Johnson's Oval Office. Grace Halsell, staff writer for Lyndon Johnson, declares in *Sacrificing Liberty* (episode IV):

> Everyone around me, without exception, was pro-Israel [she, too, at the time]. Johnson had a dozen or more close associates and aides who were both Jewish and pro-Israel. There were Walt Rostow at the White House, his brother Eugene at State, and Arthur Goldberg, Ambassador to the United Nations. Other pro-Israel advisers included Abe Fortas, Associate Justice of the Supreme Court, Democratic Party fundraiser, Abraham Feinberg, White House counsels, Leo White and Jake Jacobson. I could see the comings and goings of Abe Fortas and Arthur Goldberg, and I knew that Walt Rostow in particular, had close Israeli connections and met frequently with Israeli Embassy Minister, Ephraim "Eppy" Evron.

Walt Rostow was Johnson's National Security Advisor, while his brother Eugene was Under-Secretary of State, responsible for Near Eastern Affairs and "appointed precisely to support the coming Israeli war," according to Joan Mellen.[109] These two sons of Jewish immigrants had a good deal of control on U.S. Israeli policy. On June 8, 1967, the very day of the Israeli attack on the USS *Liberty*, Walter Rostow had recommended to Johnson that Israel be allowed to keep the captured territories. Phillip Nelson comments:

> This was a recommendation for a "sea change" in US policy since the previous clash in 1956, when Eisenhower had forced Israel, threatening economic sanctions, to return the captured territories in that skirmish. Rostow's memo became the basis for the de facto US policy subsequently assumed from that date on: Lyndon Johnson immediately acquiesced to Israel's new position.[110]

In view of Johnson's intimacy with Israeli agents and of his high treason against his own military, one may wonder if Johnson was not himself an Israeli agent, a *sayan*. This is a notion entertained unashamedly in the Jewish press. A 2013 article from the *5 Towns Jewish Times* was titled "Our First Jewish President Lyndon Johnson?" The author mentions that newly released tapes from Johnson's White House office show LBJ's "personal and often emotional connection to Israel." He recalls Johnson's continuous support of Jews and Israel in the 1940s and 50s, and mentions that, "research into Johnson's personal history indicates that he inherited his concern for the Jewish people from his family. His aunt Jessie Johnson Hatcher, a major influence on LBJ, was a member of the Zionist Organization of America." And, in an additional note: "The facts indicate that both of Lyndon Johnson's great-grandparents, on the maternal side [of his mother Rebekah Baines], were Jewish. . . . The line of Jewish mothers can be traced back three generations in Lyndon Johnson's family tree. There is little doubt that he was Jewish."[111] As a matter of fact, Johnson was the first American President to dedicate a synagogue, in Austin, five weeks after assuming office.[112]

Regardless of his genealogy, Johnson had been Israel's man ever since his Senate race in Texas in 1948, when Abraham Fortas had managed an extensive vote fraud, including 200 votes tallied in alphabetical order in the infamous Ballot Box 13. Fortas had been Johnson's primary adviser in his numerous legal quandaries, and would remain his personal attorney even after Johnson named him Supreme Court justice in 1965. Fortas would then also serve as Johnson's "back channel" to the Israeli embassy, since he was very close to Israeli Ambassador Avraham Harman (1959-68). In March 1960, Fortas hosted a breakfast meeting at his home for Israeli Prime Minister David Ben-Gurion, with Johnson as one of the featured guests.[113]

Johnson's political career had been financed by Democratic Party fundraiser Abraham Feinberg, who was also the founder in 1947 of Americans for Haganah, Inc., the biggest fundraising organization for the Jewish militia. As a consequence, Johnson had been at Israel's service from the beginning of his political life. For example, he used his position as Senate Majority Leader to oppose Eisenhower's economic sanctions against Israel after Israel's invasion of the Gaza Strip in 1956, detailing his objections in a much-publicized letter to Secretary of State John Foster Dulles.[114]

Seymour Hersh, who has a lot to say about Feinberg as the godfather of the Dimona project, writes in *The Samson Option*: "There is no question that Feinberg enjoyed the greatest presidential access and influence in his twenty years as a Jewish fundraiser and lobbyist with Lyndon Johnson. Documents at the Johnson Library show that even the most senior members of the National Security Council understood that any issue raised by Feinberg had to be answered."[115]

Another key Zionist player with whom Johnson was very close is Arthur Krim, a Hollywood mogul turned finance chairman of the Democratic Party, whose wife became Johnson's mistress under his watch. In his oral history, Krim recalls serving as President Johnson's key liaison about "the money aspect of politics. . . . I had to carry a lot of messages to him and also get things done. . . . For instance . . . [from] Abe Feinberg on what to do about Israel."[116]

The Vietnam Holocaust

Robert McNamara wrote in *In Retrospect: The Tragedy and Lessons of Vietnam* (1995): "Having reviewed the record in detail, and with the advantage of hindsight, I think it highly probable that, had President Kennedy lived, he would have pulled us out of Vietnam."[117] McNamara is in a better position than anyone else to make that judgment, and few historians today would argue against him on that point. Declassified archives prove that by October 1963, Kennedy had made up his mind to evacuate the 16,000 American military advisers whom he had reluctantly sent to Vietnam.[118]

Although Kennedy was reluctant to advertise his decision during the coming election year, he had announced his phased withdrawal plan to the National Security Council of October 2, and formalized it by National Security Action Memorandum 263, ordering the removal of "1,000 U.S. military personnel by the end of 1963," in anticipation for withdrawing "by the end of 1965 . . . the bulk of U.S. personnel."[119] On November 20, Kennedy said during a press conference that he was assessing "how we can bring Americans out of there. Now, that is our objective, to bring Americans home." Among the countless testimonies confirming Kennedy's determination for complete withdrawal, let us quote General Maxwell Taylor, head of the Joint Chiefs: "I don't recall anyone who was strongly against [sending ground troops], except one man and that was the President. The President just didn't want to be convinced that this was the right thing to do . . . It was really the President's personal conviction that U.S. ground troops shouldn't go in." General Douglas MacArthur had once told Kennedy, "Anyone wanting to commit American ground forces to the mainland of Asia should have his head examined," and according to General Taylor, this "made a hell of an impression on the President. . . . so that whenever he'd get this military advise from the Joint Chiefs or from me or anyone else, he's say, 'Well, now, you gentlemen, you go back and convince General MacArthur, then I'll be convinced."[120]

But on November 26, the day after Kennedy's funeral, Johnson buried NSAM-263 and replaced it with NSAM-273, which required the military to develop a plan "for the United States to begin carrying the war north," including "different levels of possible increased activity," and "military operations up to a line up to 50 kilometers inside Laos."[121] Johnson's decision regarding Vietnam was a clear betrayal of Kennedy's earlier policy, and the swiftness of his change suggests premeditation. Robert McNamara, continuing as Secretary of Defense, acceded to Johnson's agenda, recommending the mobilization of 50,000 soldiers and a program of "graduated overt military pressure" against North Vietnam, a policy which Johnson rubberstamped in March 1964 by memorandum NSAM-288.[122] Eventually 500,000 Americans would be sent to Vietnam.

This radical reversal of policy is a strong argument for the thesis that Kennedy was assassinated by those who wanted a Vietnam War. The question is: Who wanted a Vietnam War so bad as to assassinate the President? James Douglass and many others before him answer: CIA and Pentagon warmongers! It is certainly true that many top brasses were in favor of deepening U.S. involvement in Vietnam, and welcomed Johnson's change of policy. It is also beyond doubt that some elements of the CIA, uncontrolled by John McCone and encouraged by the treacherous ambassador Henry Cabot Lodge, were defying Kennedy's Vietnam policy and sabotaging his plan for withdrawal.

One very disturbing newspaper article has been used by James Douglass and others in support of their theory. It was published on October 2, 1963 by a journalist named Richard Starnes, serving as *Washington Daily News* correspondent in Saigon, then taken up by Arthur Krock in his daily column in the *New York Times*. Starnes stated that the CIA in Vietnam was showing an "obstinate disregard of orders, and unrestrained thirst for power." He quoted from an unnamed "high United States source" who likened the CIA's growth to "a malignancy" that he "was not sure even the White House could control any longer." The article concluded that, "If the United States ever experiences a *'Seven Days in May'* [a coup], it will come from the CIA."[123] Since Krock had been, so to speak, at the service of the Kennedys since the 1940s, it is quite possible that the whole idea of this article originated from JFK, who needed a pretext and public support to "splinter the CIA in a thousand pieces and scatter it to the winds," as he once said after the Bay of Pigs fiasco.[124] The fact that Starnes's article was published the very day of the National Security Council summoned by Kennedy, and that Kennedy specifically mentioned it then, supports this hypothesis, I think.[125] In any case, short of knowing who was Starnes's "very high official" source, it is hard to decide what to make of this short article, and it is unreasonable to give too much credit to its gloomy prediction.

No matter what CIA unruly agents were doing in Vietnam, the truth is that Johnson, not the CIA, was the leading force for intensifying U.S. military activities in Vietnam. Already in May 1961, as he returned from a visit to Vietnam at Kennedy's request, Johnson was adamant that victory required U.S. combat troops. In 1963, he opposed Kennedy's withdrawal policy behind his back, and, on November 24, two days after Kennedy's death, he summoned the ambassador to Vietnam, Henry Cabot Lodge, to tell him, "I am not going to be the president who saw Southeast Asia go the way China went."[126] No one had had to convince or pressure him, between the 22nd and the 24th of November. The decision was his.

And so, although Johnson's reversal of policy is consistent with the thesis that "the CIA killed Kennedy" — as Fletcher Prouty argued in *The CIA, Vietnam, and the Plot to Assassinate John F. Kennedy*[127] — it fits better the "Johnson killed Kennedy" thesis.

But why did Johnson want a Vietnam War? Was it the typical war profiteer's greed? Soon before taking over the White House, Johnson had invested in the Dallas aircraft manufacturer Ling-Temco-Vought, which was to become one of the Pentagon's biggest arms suppliers for the Vietnam War.[128] Or was it just the crude love of war of a megalomaniac personality? During an informal conversation with journalists, to the insisting question "Why are we in Vietnam?" "LBJ unzipped his fly, drew out his substantial organ and declared, 'This is why!'"[129]

There must be something else. Whatever Johnson's personal reasons, they cannot explain everything. Who then, beside Johnson, was strongly pushing for war? The name that first comes up is Walt Rostow, Johnson's National Security Advisor.

Originally brought into the White House by JFK, who had made him deputy to the National Security Advisor McGeorge Bundy, Rostow had already weighted heavily on Kennedy's decision to send military personnel to Vietnam, as David Halberstam shows in his study on the role of intellectuals in the Vietnam War (*The Best and the Brightest*, 1972). But Kennedy had grown weary of his bellicose advise ("Walt had ten ideas, nine of which would lead to disaster," he is quoted as saying).[130] Rostow was promoted by Johnson and found in him more enthusiasm for his war plans. According to John Galbraith, a former Kennedy adviser, Rostow was the main promoter of the lie that Johnson's Vietnam policy was a continuation of Kennedy's, "beginning in 1967 with a thick compilation for Johnson himself of Kennedy's public statements on Vietnam policy and continuing into the 1990s."[131]

Support for the Vietnam War also came from the early neoconservatives. It was under Johnson that Norman Podhoretz, editor-in-chief of *Commentary* (the magazine of the *American Jewish Committee*), turned from anti-imperialist activist to war-monger. He explained this turning point in his 1979 book *Breaking Ranks*: "American support for Israel depended upon continued American involvement in international affairs — from which it followed that an American withdrawal into the kind of isolationist mood . . . represented a direct threat to the security of Israel."[132]

Meanwhile, by a dialectical process often observed in Jewish intellectual history, other Jews stirred a loud and strong popular opposition to the Vietnam War. With the leaking of the *Pentagon Papers* by Daniel Ellsberg, helped by Anthony Russo, Noam Chomsky and Howard Zinn (all Jewish by birth), the protest movement mobilized the American youth, who was simultaneously made totally insensitive and almost unaware of Israel's war of aggression and illegal occupation of Palestinian territories.

The Vietnam War was good for Israel, not only because it intensified the Cold War and therefore U.S. hostility to Egypt, but also because it focused popular attention and indignation to the Far East rather than to the Middle East. Zionists working for Greater Israel surely understood that the capacity of the U.S. administration to condemn Israel's aggression and crimes would be much diminished if the U.S. had worse crimes to be blamed for. As paradoxical as it seems, the Vietnam War shielded Israel from too much pressure from America and from the rest of the world.

This didn't escape French President Charles De Gaulle. In a press conference on November 27, 1967, after condemning Israel's aggression and famously designating "the Jews" as "an elite people, sure of themselves and domineering," he called for the four great powers to enforce an international settlement on the basis of Israel's withdrawal from the occupied territories, and then added:

> But one cannot see how such an agreement can be reached as long as one of the greatest among the four will not withdraw from the heinous war that they are waging elsewhere. . . . Without the tragedy of Vietnam, the conflict between Israel and the Arabs would not have become what it has become. And if South-East Asia could experience a renewal of peace, the Middle-East would also find its way to peace, in the climate of détente which would follow such an event.[133]

A "climate of détente", therefore, was the last thing Israel wanted. Nasser commented after this press conference: "De Gaulle is the only head of state on whose friendship the Arabs can count," adding in February 1968 that under his leadership "France has adopted a position compliant with justice and peace."[134] But three months later, De Gaulle became the target of a major student protest led by predominantly Jewish activists,[135] that ultimately forced De Gaulle to resign.

Strangely, it is during the Vietnam War that the term "Holocaust" became a common designation of the killing of Jews during World War II. It is absurd: Hitler was not working for the glory of Yahweh — unless we believe, like rabbi Moshe Shonfeld, that "The Zionist leaders saw the spilt Jewish blood of the Holocaust as grease for the wheels of the Jewish national state."[136] But the term logically applies much better to the Vietnam War, if we consider that by focusing the attention of the American public, it left the field to Israel for its conquest of Palestinian territories — Yahweh's promised land.

I know that some readers will find the very idea preposterous. But all I'm saying is what De Gaulle said: Israel profited from the Vietnam War. I am not suggesting that Israel killed Kennedy for the sole purpose of having a Vietnam War, only that Israel had as much interest in escalating and prolonging the war as anyone else.

How Johnson became Vice-President

Why did Kennedy choose Johnson as Vice-President? That choice went against the wish of almost his all campaign team. To his brother Bobby and Kenneth O'Donnell, who were trying to reverse his decision, John explained that Johnson would be less dangerous as Vice-President than as Senate Majority Leader. Besides, "I'm forty-three years old, and I'm the healthiest candidate for President in the United States. . . . I'm not going to die in office. So the Vice-Presidency doesn't mean anything."[137]

To his assistant Hyman Raskin, he apologized: "You know, we had never considered Lyndon, but I was left with no choice . . . those bastards [Johnson and his ally Sam Rayburn] were trying to frame me. They threatened me with problems and I don't need more problems."[138] He never explained the terms of the blackmail, and nobody knows for sure JFK's compelling reason to choose LBJ as his running mate. O'Donnell and Powers conclude their chapter "How Lyndon got on the ticket" with this revealing anecdote: when a campaign volunteer, in despair, asked Kennedy, "What will I say to all my friends in Boston when they ask me why you picked Lyndon Johnson?" he smiled and said, "Pretend you know something they don't know."[139] This is echoed by Pierre Salinger, who got this answer to the same question: "The whole story will never be known. And it's just as well that it won't be."[140]

However, it is on record, thanks to Kennedy insiders such as Kenneth O'Donnell or Arthur Schlesinger, that it was in fact Philip Graham and Joseph Alsop, respectively publisher and main columnist of the *Washington Post*, who convinced Kennedy to take Johnson on his ticket, in a closed door conversation. Schlesinger states that Kennedy's final decision "defies historical reconstruction" — a curious statement for a historian so well informed.[141] Alan Hart has filled in the blanks: since both Graham and Alsop were strongly pro-Israel as well as pro-Johnson, and since both could exert a huge influence on public opinion, Hart infers that, "Kennedy was forced by Israel's supporters to take Johnson as his vice-presidential running mate."[142]

It is interesting that the official biographer of Katherine Graham, Deborah Davis, includes Joseph Alsop among the *Washington Post* staffers who were "owned" by the CIA through its Operation Mockingbird.[143] Let's recall that Katherine Graham was the daughter and heir of Eugene Meyer, who had purchased the *Washington Post* in 1933 while a member of the influential American Jewish Committee. It is not only ironical but typical that Graham would, through her biographer, emphasize the CIA's "control" over American mainstream news in the 1960s, while saying nothing of the foreign interests that exerted a much greater control through her own family.

Johnson, the mastermind

With the attempted sinking of the USS *Liberty*, there is clear evidence that Johnson was willing to betray his own country and sacrifice hundreds of Americans for Israel's war of aggression and expansion. It is therefore natural to ask: Was the Kennedy assassination also part of Johnson's deal with the Zionists?

Many Americans immediately suspected Johnson's involvement in the Dallas coup, especially in Texas, where his reputation for corruption and murder was well established. In 1964, James Evetts Haley's book *A Texan Looks at Lyndon* brought Johnson's epic corruption to national attention. Although at that time Americans received no sign that the Kennedy family suspected Johnson, many indications have since surfaced that this was the case. Eddie Fisher mentions in his 1999 autobiography that, while flying back to Washington from Dallas the day after the assassination, together with Jackie Kennedy's press secretary, Pamela Turnure, his then lover, "Pam told me, Jackie Kennedy told her, 'Lyndon Johnson did it.' Words I'll never forget.'"[144] Jackie never voiced her suspicion publicly, but merely mentioned in her oral history recorded in 1964 by Arthur Schlesinger Jr. (released in 2011): "Jack said it to me sometimes. He said, 'Oh, God, can you ever imagine what would happen to the country if Lyndon was president.'"[145] What happened to the country is for Americans to see.

Although I am not aware of any unequivocal record of it, it is generally believed that Robert Kennedy also suspected Johnson. There had always been a deep antipathy between the two men. "Johnson lies all the time," RFK would say, "he just lies continuously, about everything. In every conversation I have with him, he lies . . . he lies even when he doesn't have to."[146]

From the side of Johnson's entourage, incriminating testimonies have also surfaced, although they are hard to verify. Madeleine Brown, who claimed to have been Johnson's mistress for 20 years and to have born his child, wrote about Johnson's foreknowledge of the assassination in her book *Texas in the Morning* (1997), and repeated in front of cameras what Johnson had told her November 21, 1963: "Tomorrow those goddamn

Kennedys will never embarrass me again; that's no threat, that's a promise."[147] In 1984, Billie Sol Estes, a Texas businessman who had funneled hundreds of thousands of dollars to Johnson in the 50s, tried to negotiate leniency from the Department of Justice in exchange for information on five killings ordered by Johnson, including Johnson's own sister Josefa. He also shared with investigator William Reymond his conviction that Johnson orchestrated the assassination of Kennedy.[148] One of the most convincing cases against Johnson has been made by Barr McClellan, a lawyer working for the law firm of Johnson's attorney Edward Clark, in his book *Blood, Money & Power: How LBJ Killed JFK* (2003).

Several Kennedy investigators have identified Lyndon Johnson as the mastermind of the assassination. The most impressive case has been made in more than 700 pages by Phillip Nelson in *LBJ: The Mastermind of JFK's Assassination* (2010), and two other books deserve mention: Roger Stone, *The Man Who Killed Kennedy: The Case Against LBJ* (2013); and James Tague, *LBJ and the Kennedy Killing* (2013).[149] Stone and Tague, however, ignore Johnson's intimate connection with Israel, while Nelson has started connecting the dots in his sequel *LBJ: From Mastermind to "The Colossus"* (2014), and in *Remember the Liberty!: Almost Sunk by Treason on the High Seas* (2017).

Nelson portrays Johnson as a manipulative psychopath and a serial killer whose single aim had always been the presidency. He draws from previous biographers such as Robert Caro, for whom Johnson was a man thirsting "for power in its most naked form, for power not to improve the lives of others, but to manipulate and dominate them, to bend them to his will, . . . a hunger so fierce and consuming that no consideration of morality or ethics, no cost to himself — or to anyone else — could stand before it."[150]

It needs to be emphasized that Johnson was implicated in three corruption scandals dating back to his tenure as Texan senator. In November 1963, one of his Texan accomplices, Navy Secretary Fred Korth, resigned after RFK's Justice Department implicated him in a fraud for a $7 billion contract given illegally to the Texan company General Dynamics (the TFX/F-111 project). Johnson's personal secretary Bobby Baker ("my strong right arm", he called him), was charged in the same case. Baker's indictment made the headlines of the weekly magazine *Life,* just days before November 22: "The Bombshell Bobby Baker: . . . Scandal grows and grows in

Washington."[151] One of Baker's longtime business associates, insurance agent Don Reynolds, was testifying against him on November 22 before the Senate Rules Committee; he attested to having seen Baker with a suitcase containing $100,000 for "payoff to Johnson for his role in securing the Fort Worth TFX contract" (as Baker later confirmed). Later, Reynolds would voice his conviction that LBJ was implicated in JFK's assassination, and on January 24, 1964, he stated to the FBI that, once "Baker stated while referring to the swearing in of Kennedy, words to the effect that the s.o.b is being sworn in, but he will never live his term out. He will die a violent death."[152]

Because of this mounting scandal and other suspicions of corruption, Kennedy had resolved to change Vice-President for his upcoming reelection campaign, according to Kennedy's longtime secretary Evelyn Lincoln (*Kennedy and Johnson,* 1968, a short but very interesting testimony to the growing alienation of Johnson from Kennedy's government, as well as Johnson's efforts to make it appear otherwise).[153] Richard Nixon, who happened to be in Dallas the day before the President's visit, leaked the rumor to the *Dallas Morning News,* which reported on November 22nd: "Nixon Predicts JFK May Drop Johnson." Instead, Johnson became President that very day.

Nixon certainly suspected Johnson's guilt in the assassination. He hinted at it when he said in front of a camera, tongue-in-cheek: "You know LBJ, he never likes to be number 2."[154] Roger Stone, a former Nixon assistant and the author of *The Man Who Killed Kennedy: The Case Against LBJ,* claims that, in his presence, Nixon identified Jack Ruby (Oswald's killer) as one of "Johnson's boys."[155] I doubt that story: Stone could have made it up to counter another rumor about Ruby's connection to Nixon, sparked by a forged 1947 FBI memo stating that "one Jack Rubenstein of Chicago . . . is performing information functions for the staff of Congressman Richard Nixon."[156]

Nevertheless, there is another link between Ruby and Johnson. Ruby unequivocally pointed to Johnson as the mastermind of the plot when, at the end of a short filmed news conference in the Dallas County Jail in March 1965, he declared in front of cameras, "When I mentioned about Adlai Stevenson, if he was Vice-President there would never have been an assassination of our beloved President Kennedy." Asked to explain what he meant, Ruby continued, "Well the answer is the man in office now."[157] It seems that Ruby, by that time, felt betrayed by Johnson, whom he had expected to pardon him (Ruby's defense was that he had killed Oswald out of love for the Kennedys).

That Ruby expected to be vindicated by Johnson transpires from his testimony to Warren Commission members (including Warren himself), on June 7, 1964. Ruby pleaded to be given a chance to talk directly to Johnson: "If you don't take me back to Washington tonight to give me a chance to prove to the President that I am not guilty, then you will see the most tragic thing that will ever happen." He added that "maybe something can be saved . . . if our President, Lyndon Johnson, knew the truth from me."[158] This can be interpreted as a veiled threat addressed to Johnson. Ruby, who by this time had been sentenced to death, may have been trying to remind Johnson that his contract included a presidential pardon. Even more curiously, Ruby hinted in his deposition that the Jewish community could suffer if he spoke: "There will be a certain tragic occurrence happening if you don't take my testimony and somehow vindicate me so my people don't suffer because of what I have done." He feared, he said, that his act would be used "to create some falsehood about some of the Jewish faith."[159] All Ruby got out of his confused testimony was a second pointless Warren Commission interview one month later (July 18, 1964), this time by none other than Arlen Specter. [160] His frustration would explain why in March 1965, Ruby finally accused Johnson in veiled words. Shortly thereafter, he wrote a sixteen-page letter that he managed to smuggle out of jail, accusing Johnson and calling him "a Nazi of the worst order."[161] By doing so, he probably speeded his own death, on January 3, 1967.

All this is at best circumstantial evidence of a connection between Johnson and Ruby. However, there is one indisputable fact that should be given proper consideration: Ruby and Johnson are the only two persons known to have taken steps to make sure that Oswald was silenced forever. Because Ruby could only shoot one bullet at Oswald — he had planned to shoot three, he declared —, Oswald was still alive when taken to Dallas Parkland Hospital.

Dr. Charles Crenshaw recalls in his book *JFK, Conspiracy of Silence* (1992) that, while operating on Oswald with other surgeons, he noticed that an unknown man looking like Oliver Hardy with a pistol hanging from his back pocket had entered the operation room. Minutes later, he was told about an urgent call for him and left the operating room to take it. The call was from the newly sworn President Lyndon Johnson who first asked "Dr. Crenshaw, how is the accused assassin?" Crenshaw answered: "Mr. President, he's holding his own at the moment." Then Johnson said firmly: "Dr. Crenshaw, I want a deathbed confession from the accused assassin. There's a man in the operating room who will take the statement. I will expect full cooperation in this matter." Dr. Crenshaw answered "Yes, sir," and hung up. Thirty years later, he comments: "As I stood there in a state of disbelief, my mind was racing. First, 'deathbed confession' implies that someone is going to die. If Oswald doesn't die on the table, is 'Oliver Hardy' or someone else going to kill him?" Since Dr. Crenshaw had just told Johnson that Oswald was "holding his own," the expression "deathbed confession" did sound like an implicit order that Oswald should not leave the operating room alive. It seems that Johnson wanted Ruby's job finished. Moments after Dr. Crenshaw went back to the operating room, Oswald's heartbeat stopped: "Oliver Hardy" disappeared, never to be seen again. "The incident," wrote Crenshaw, "confounded logic. Why the President of the United States would get personally involved in the investigation of the assassination, or why he would take the inquest out of the hands of the Texas authorities was perplexing."[162]

CHAPTER 4
Jack Ruby, Gangster for Zion

By a strange paradox, Kennedy researchers who stand by the CIA-Pentagon conspiracy theory build much of their case on the biography of Oswald, while at the same time claiming that Oswald had little or nothing to do with the killing. If Oswald was "just a patsy," as he claimed to be, the quest for the real culprits must logically begin by investigating the man who shot Oswald at pointblank in the stomach at 11:21 a.m. on November 24 in the Dallas Police Station, thereby sealing the possibility that a trial would draw attention to the inconsistencies of the charge against him, and perhaps expose the real perpetrators.

Short of identifying the snipers who shot Kennedy, the background of the man who shot the patsy is the most important information to start from in our search for the chief plotters. Therefore, one would normally expect Jack Ruby to be the most investigated character by Kennedy researchers. But that is not the case.

Of course, it is perfectly natural that Chief Justice Earl Warren, when Ruby told him on June 7, 1964, "I have been used for a purpose," failed to ask him who had used him and for what purpose.[163] But what about Kennedy researchers? Are only readers of the *Forward* ("News That Matters To American Jews") worthy of being informed that "Lee Harvey Oswald's Killer 'Jack Ruby' Came From Strong Jewish Background," and that he told his rabbi Hillel Silverman that he "did it for the Jewish people"? Here is the relevant passage of Steve North's 2013 article, relating Silverman's reaction after hearing on the radio that a "Jack Rubenstein" had killed the assassin:

> "I was shocked," said Silverman. "I visited him the next day in jail, and I said, 'Why, Jack, why?' He said, 'I did it for the American people.'" I interrupted Silverman, pointing out that other reports had Ruby saying he did it "to show that Jews had guts." The rabbi sighed. "Yes, he mentioned that," Silverman said. "But I don't like to mention it. I think he said, 'I did it for the Jewish people.' But I've tried to wipe that statement from my mind."[164]

Ruby's defense lawyer William Kunstler also claims in his memoir that Ruby told him: "I did it for the Jews," repeating on several occasions: "I did this that they wouldn't implicate Jews." During Kunstler's last visit Ruby handed him a note in which he reiterated that his motive was to "protect American Jews from a pogrom that could occur because of anger over the assassination."[165] There is only one possible interpretation of Ruby's words: he must have known, and those you sent him to kill Oswald must have known, that if Oswald had been trialed, the Jewish hand in JFK's assassination would likely have been made visible.

Why is this crucial information not in any book on the Kennedy assassination? James Douglass, to take just one example, insists, without a shred of evidence, that Ruby, besides being a "Chicago mob functionary," was "CIA-connected" (while smuggling guns for Castro!)[166] He never mentions his strong Jewish background, and only gives his real name in a single endnote quoting another author. Could Douglass's strange omission have the same motive as Ruby's murder of Oswald, namely to "protect American Jews from a pogrom that could occur because of anger over the assassination"?

Ruby is not the only person connected to Oswald whose confused words implicating "the Jews" are carefully concealed from the public. On March 29, 1977, George DeMohrenschildt, a Russian geologist who had befriended Oswald in Dallas in 1962 at the request of CIA agent J. Walton Moore, was found dead with a bullet through his head. His death was ruled a suicide, but the Sherriff's report mentions that in his last months he complained that "the Jews" and "the Jewish mafia" were out to get him.[167] His wife confirmed to Jim Marrs, author of *Crossfire: The Plot that Killed Kennedy* (1989), that her husband thought that "the Jewish Mafia and the FBI" were out to get him.[168] Most people who have heard about DeMohrenschildt have never heard this intriguing detail.

After DeMohrenschildt moved away from Dallas in June 1963, Oswald was chaperoned by Ruth Paine, who found him a job at the Texas School Book Depository, where he started working on October 16.[169] It is generally assumed that Ruth Paine did this on behalf of the CIA, but I have been unable to find the origin of that claim. I was surprised, however, to read in her testimony to the Warren Commission that in 1950, Ruth Paine had been "a leader in the Jewish community at Indianapolis," and that in 1954-55, she worked with a group which "consisted of people over the age of 60, all of them Jewish" — "a good many of them had come from Kiev," "and they spoke Yiddish in conducting their business meetings."[170] Although converted to Quakerism, Ruth Paine was obviously very much connected to the Dallas Jewish community.

To come back to Jack Ruby, I know of only one book presenting serious research about him: Seth Kantor's *Who Was Jack Ruby?* (1978, retitled *The Ruby Cover-Up* in 1980). Kantor was a reporter working for the *Dallas Times Herald* in 1963. He knew Ruby and was less than ten feet away from him when Ruby shot Oswald, as he reported the same day.

Although, in its final report, the Warren Commission declared that it could "not establish a significant link between Ruby and organized crime," because "Ruby has disclaimed that he was associated with organized criminal activities, and law enforcement agencies have confirmed that denial,"[171] there is plenty of evidence of Ruby's association with organized crime. G. Robert Blakey, chief counsel for the House Select Committee on Assassinations from 1977 to 1979, said: "The most plausible explanation for the murder of Oswald by Jack Ruby was that Ruby had stalked him on behalf of organized crime, trying to reach him on at least three occasions in the forty-eight hours before he silenced him forever."[172] Implicating "organized crime" in the JFK assassination was, of course, the least damaging conclusion that the HSCA could come up with, short of ridiculing itself by confirming the *Warren Report*. The phrase "damage control" is appropriate here. "Organized crime" was just perfect for a *Washington Post* headline: "Mobsters Linked to JFK Death."[173]

Gangsters for Zion

Most Americans, hearing that Jack Ruby was a Chicago mobster, must have imagined he was Sicilian, or perhaps Corsican. Most have never heard that his real name was Jacob Leon Rubenstein, and that he was the son of Jewish Polish immigrants. The truth is, Jacob Rubenstein was part of the Jewish mafia. He had moved from Chicago to Dallas in 1947, soon after 15 other Chicago mobsters (3 Italian and 9 Jewish) who had settled there to take over the prostitution business. That's when he changed his name from Rubenstein to Ruby. Ruby's mentor and role model was Mickey Cohen, who was also in Chicago during the Prohibition but operated mainly in Hollywood afterwards. During his trial for shooting Oswald, Ruby's legal team was fronted by Melvin Belli, a longtime friend and attorney of Cohen (Belli's line was that Ruby had suffered temporary insanity due to a bout with "psychomotor epilepsy").[174] Cohen had himself followed in the footsteps of Benjamin "Bugsy" Siegelbaum, co-founder of Murder Incorporated. Both Cohen and Siegelbaum worked under Meyer Lansky (born Suchowljansky), the most powerful Jewish mafia boss, who had made a fortune with his Havana casinos and brothels, of which he was dispossessed by Castro in 1959. Lansky's biographer Hank Messick describes him as the head of the National Crime Syndicate. "Thanks largely to Lansky, organized crime has changed from an ugly growth on the body politic capable of being removed by surgery to a cancerous part of our economic and political systems."[175]

Mickey Cohen claims in his memoirs that, in the 1940s and 1950s, he was "engrossed with Israel." He boasts about his contributions to the arms-trafficking of the Haganah. Gary Wean, a detective sergeant for the Los Angeles Police Department, claims in *There's a Fish in the Courthouse* (1987) that he saw Ruby twice in Hollywood in 1946 and 1947 in the presence of Cohen.[176] He also writes that Cohen "spent a lot of time" with Menachem Begin,[177] and that he was sharing his girlfriend, stripper Candy Barr, with Begin as well as Ruby.[178]

Cohen's work for Israel was part of large network. A pact had been sealed between prominent Zionists and Jewish mafia bosses around 1945, when the Haganah organized a highly effective black market of weapons and explosives from the U.S. to Palestine. Abraham Feinberg, with whom readers are now familiar, was deeply involved in this operation, as founder of Americans for Haganah, Inc.[179] The buying and smuggling of arms were orchestrated by a group of about 40 wealthy American Jews who pledged to help David Ben-Gurion when the latter visited New York in July 1945. The group acted under the legal cover of a charity, the Sonneborn Institute, officially headed by Rudolf Sonneborn. Its story is told by Leonard Slater in *The Pledge* (Simon & Schuster, 1970). The group operated separately from the Jewish Agency in order to shield it from direct involvement in unlawful activities. Among its active members was the future Jerusalem mayor (1965-93) Teddy Kollek, who also played a key role in forging the CIA-Mossad Alliance.[180]

Robert Rockaway has documented the contribution of the Jewish underworld to Zionism in an article "Gangsters for Zion: How Jewish mobsters helped Israel gain its independence." He writes:

> In 1945, the Jewish Agency, the pre-state Israeli government headed by David Ben-Gurion, created a vast clandestine arms-purchasing-and-smuggling network throughout the United States. The operation was placed under the aegis of the Haganah, the

underground forerunner of the Israel Defense Forces, and involved hundreds of Americans from every walk of life. . . . One group, who remained anonymous and rarely talked about, were men who were tough, streetwise, unafraid, and had access to ready cash: Jewish gangsters.

Sent by Ben-Gurion to the U.S. to purchase heavy armaments, Haganah operative Yehuda Arazi approached Meyer Lansky and met with members of Murder Incorporated. Another Haganah emissary, Reuvin Dafni, who would become Israeli consul in Los Angeles and New York, also dealt with Jewish gangsters. "When I interviewed Dafni," Rockaway writes, "he told me about his meetings with Jewish mobsters. His meetings were arranged by members of the local Jewish community. His first meeting was in Miami with Sam Kay, a leading Miami Jewish gangster." Dafni also met with Bugsy Siegel (Siegelbaum):

As Dafni relates, "I told him my story, how the Haganah was raising money to buy weapons with which to fight. When I finished, Siegel asked, 'You mean to tell me Jews are fighting?' Yes, I replied. Then Siegel, who was sitting across the table, leaned forward till his nose was almost touching mine. 'You mean fighting, as in killing?' Yes, I answered. Siegel leaned back, looked at me for a moment and said, 'OK, I'm with you.' . . . From then on," recalled Dafni, "every week I got a phone call to go to the restaurant. And every week I received a suitcase filled with $5 and $10 bills. The payments continued till I left Los Angeles." Dafni estimates that Siegel gave him a total of $50,000.

Some of those "gangsters for Zion", Rockaway writes, "did so out of ethnic loyalties," or "saw themselves as defenders of the Jews, almost biblical-like fighters. It was part of their self-image."[181]

Such is the background of Jack Ruby. His arms-smuggling activities are well documented, but the fact that they were for the benefit of Israel is often blurred. Allan Weberman refers to Ruby and other mobsters' arms-dealing and in *Coup d'État in America* (1975), but makes no mention of their Jewishness (unless being "strongly anti-Nazi" counts as a synonym), and claims that they were in fact arming Castro — while simultaneously participating in plots to kill him.[182]

Ruby knew Lewis McWillie, the manager of Meyer and Jake Lansky's Tropicana nightclub casino in Havana. After Castro's overthrow of Batista in January 1959, Meyer Lansky relocated to Miami, but Jake Lansky was arrested and confined to a luxury prison, the Trescornia detention camp, together with another mafia figure, Santo Trafficante Jr., who, although non-Jewish, had sworn allegiance to the Lansky brothers, and controlled substantial portions of Havana's gambling and prostitution rackets. While in prison, Jake Lansky and Trafficante were often visited by Lewis McWillie, who was negotiating their release by Castro. Ruby told the Warren Commission that he visited McWillie in 1959 in Havana, and that he knew McWillie's bosses, whom he referred to as "the Fox brothers, the greatest that have been expelled from Cuba."[183] (McWillie would later acknowledge to the HSCA that "Jack Ruby could have been out there [Havana] one time with me.") Ruby added that McWillie and one of the Fox-Lansky brothers later visited him in Dallas.[184]

In addition, Kantor quotes from a classified message that was sent from CIA headquarters to National Security Advisor McGeorge Bundy on November 28, 1963, indicating that, according to an informer, an "'American gangster-type named Ruby' visited Cuba around 1959" where he met frequently with "an American gangster gambler named Santos who was in prison." Santos turned out to be an assumed name of Santo Trafficante Jr.

The interesting part is that, in September 1962, Trafficante is reported to have said to José Alman, a prominent member of the Cuban exile community in Miami, that, "President Kennedy would get what was coming to him." Aleman disagreed and argued that Kennedy would be reelected. "No, José," said Trafficante. "He is going to be hit." When Trafficante was asked by Richard Sprague of the HSCA, "did you ever discuss with any individuals plans to assassinate President Kennedy prior to his assassination?" Trafficante refused to answer.[185]

Jack Ruby was in close contact with his fellow mobsters in 1963, as Kantor shows in great detail (without underscoring their particular ethnicity):

> [Ruby had] private, hotline phone conversations with the underworld at two crucial intervals. The first of these intervals was in June, 1963, when a group of Chicago gangsters held a clandestine council in Dallas to plan the takeover of local gambling and prostitution operations. The second interval covered the 11 days just before President Kennedy's assassination, when Ruby abruptly signed a power of attorney, giving up certain rights to control his own money. He also suddenly bought and installed a safe for the first time in his 16 years as a Dallas nightclub operator, to store extra amounts of money.[186]

By June 8, "a large group of Chicago racketeers began to show up at Ruby's Carousel and at two other nearby strip-show clubs, according to a confidential report to Dallas Police Chief Jesse E. Curry by Lieutenant Robert L. May Jr., who had been head of the vice squad."[187]

On November 11, Ruby met in Dallas with Alex Gruber, who was known for his connections with Mickey Cohen. Gruber, who had not visited Ruby in years, told the FBI that he was in Joplin, Missouri at that time, and had simply decided to drop in on Ruby "since Dallas, Texas, was about 100 miles from Joplin" (the distance is 360 miles).[188] In the afternoon of November 22, Ruby phoned Alex Gruber in Los Angeles. "Gruber subsequently told the FBI he didn't really know why Ruby called."[189] That's when Ruby may have received an offer he couldn't refuse. As mentioned earlier, he was probably told the precise moment of Oswald's transfer by PR man Sam Bloom, whose name, address and phone number were later found at his home.[190]

In an apparent attempt to make it impossible for him to do what was expected of him, Ruby warned anonymously the Dallas Police: Lieutenant Billy Grammer, whose statement can be heard on YouTube, received a phone call at 3 a.m. on November 24 from a man who knew Grammer's name, and whose voice sounded familiar to Grammer although he could not then put a name on it. The caller told Grammer that he knew of the plan to move Oswald from the basement and that unless the plan was changed, "we are going to kill him." After Oswald was shot and Ruby arrested, Grammer recognized Ruby as the caller.[191]

Ruby and the Dallas Police

When Ruby shot Oswald on Sunday November 24, this was not the first time he had been allowed into the Dallas Police Station. Ruby knew just about every policeman in town, and was as often hanging around the Police Station as the policemen were at his strip club, the Carousel. "I have always been very close to the police department, I don't know why," he told the Warren Commission. Surely he knew why but couldn't tell. Friendship with the Dallas policemen was his mob assignment, and it was the reason why he was chosen for silencing Oswald: few people had as much ease in making their way into the Police Station.

Ruby spent a lot of time from Friday 22 to Sunday 24 at the Dallas Police Station, making several attempt to enter room 317 on the third floor where Oswald was interrogated. Shortly after 7 p.m. on Friday, the day Kennedy was assassinated and Oswald arrested, Kantor writes,

> John Rutledge, a veteran police reporter for *The Dallas Morning News,* saw Jack Ruby, whom he easily recognized by sight, step from a public elevator onto the third floor. Ruby was between two men who wore lapel credentials identifying them as out-of-town reporters. The three walked rapidly past a police officer stationed at the elevators to keep out anyone not on official business. Ruby was hunched over, writing something on a piece of paper and then showing it to one of the reporters as they walked toward Room 317, where Oswald was being interrogated by Captain Fritz and others. . . . A guard was posted at the bureau door to keep reporters from getting in to use the phones, but Ruby had no trouble easing in. He knew the guard. Ruby walked in and shook hands with Eberhardt, who asked him what he was doing.[192]

Here is the relevant part from the deposition of Detective August M. Eberhardt to the Warren Commission:

> Mr. EBERHARDT. He came in and said hello to me, shook hands with me. I asked him what he was doing. He told me he was a translator for the newspapers. Of course, I knew that he could speak Yiddish. Had a notebook in his hand . . . I do remember him taking his notebook and hitting his lapel, and he said, "I am here as a reporter," and he took the notebook and hit like that.
>
> Mr. GRIFFIN. Do you know if there were Israeli newspaper or Yiddish—
>
> Mr. EBERHARDT. There was a bunch of them running around there talking that unknown tongue. I don't know what they were saying.[193]

What a shame these Yiddish-speaking reporters who needed Ruby to translate for them were not traced and identified.

Victor Robertson Jr., a reporter for WFAA radio and TV in Dallas, also testified seeing Ruby attempting to enter room 317 while Oswald was in there. Despite those testimonies, the Commission denied that Ruby was ever on the third floor of the Police Station on Friday evening.

Later that same day, after a short visit to the synagogue, Ruby bought a dozen corned beef sandwiches and telephoned detective Richard M. Sims to offer delivering the free food right to the office. Sims declined, but Ruby found another reason to go anyway and, at about 11:30 p.m., he was seen on the third floor again. That was precisely when "Police Chief Jesse E. Curry and District Attorney Henry M. Wade appeared in the corridor with an announcement that Oswald would be put on display in the basement police assembly room for all to see." The press conference was held around midnight.[194]

Ruby, naturally, was there, as several witnesses testified and as a photo proves.[195] The Warren Commission admitted Ruby's presence, but the Warren Report portrayed Ruby simply as a casual bystander. "Nowhere in its 888-page report to the public did the Commission include Ruby's admission to the FBI, a month after the crime, that he was carrying a loaded, sub-nosed revolver in his right-hand pocket during the Oswald press session in the assembly room." Ruby couldn't approach Oswald close enough, as the room was packed with reporters and photographers.[196]

The next day, Saturday 23, Ruby brought sandwiches to reporters in the police press room. Kantor writes:

> Other reliable outside witnesses reported seeing Ruby or talking with him at intervals during Saturday afternoon — witnesses such as Jeremiah A. O'Leary Jr. of *The Washington Star* and Thayer Waldo, a reporter to *The Fort Worth Star-Telegram.* Waldo met Ruby in the third-floor corridor, talked with him and was handed a Carousel card by Ruby after 4 p.m. Yet the Warren Commission said it could reach "no firm conclusion as to whether or not Ruby visited the Dallas police department on Saturday" because "no police officer has reported Ruby's presence on that day" and because "Ruby has not mentioned such a visit." In other words, the Warren Commission decided there had been no conspiracy between Dallas police officers and Jack Ruby because none of them reported it at the time.[197]

At 9:30 on Sunday morning, Oswald was removed from his fifth-floor cell and taken down the jail elevator to the third floor, where Captain Fritz would question him again. Then arrangements were made for the transfer of Oswald to the County Jail. A little after 10:30, Kantor hypothesizes, "a call was placed to the unlisted phone in Ruby's apartment; Ruby was told where to enter the station and that the transfer van was en route."[198] Ruby first went to the Western Union office in the next block, and arrived just in time to see Oswald being transferred. This narrow timing has been used as evidence that there could be no premeditation and therefore no conspiracy. But Kantor theorizes that Ruby's entrance into the Police Station using the public stairway to the basement jail office area "could have triggered the go-ahead signal for Oswald to be brought down," and he produces plausible evidence that it did. The way Ruby entered the station is still unclear, but the HSCA voted in 1979 that it had come to believe that "it was less likely that Ruby entered the police station without assistance."[199]

Conclusion

There can be no doubt that Jack Ruby's shooting of Oswald was premeditated, and there is a strong suspicion that it was done with complicity within the Dallas Police. Ruby didn't act on his own, but, as he said to a deaf Warren Commission, he "was used for a purpose." As his former girlfriend and nightclub dancer Gail Raven once said: "He had no choice. . . . Jack had bosses, just like everyone else."[200] We have a very clear picture of who his bosses were: Gangsters for Zion.

We are now starting to get an overall picture of the Zionist criminal network that organized Kennedy's assassination in Dallas. It includes powerful Jewish figures in politics and business, as well as Irgun-connected gangsters, all devoted to Israel.

Lyndon Johnson and his sponsor Abraham Feinberg, in close contact with Tel Aviv, seem to be pulling the main strings, while businessmen of Dallas Citizens Council prepared the ambush locally. Abraham Zapruder was tasked with filming the event — and his camera didn't shake as shots were fired from close behind him. He looked satisfied when interviewed on TV two hours later.[201]

If everything had gone according to plan, Kennedy's head would have been hit from the back by a bullet fired from the Dal-Tex building, which would have made it easy to incriminate Oswald working in the School Book Depository next to the Dal-Tex. But the primary sniper missed, forcing the backup team to shoot the fatal bullet from the "grassy knoll," hitting Kennedy's skull from the front. Hence the need to tamper the Zapruder film and keep it locked for 12 years. Hence also the need to steal Kennedy's body from Dallas's Parkland Hospital and manufacture a fake autopsy in Washington's Naval Bethesda Hospital. Hence also the need to promptly wash and fix, before any examination by the FBI, the Lincoln Continental limousine that had carried Kennedy to his death, and had bullet holes in its windshield.[202]

Another thing went wrong: the plan was to shoot Oswald in the confusion of his arrest in a movie theater in the afternoon of November 22, and it can be plausibly assumed that this was a job for Ruby.[203] It was unfortunate for the conspirators that he missed the chance and that Oswald had time to claim his innocence in front of cameras ("I didn't shoot anybody . . . I'm just a patsy"). Oswald had to be killed anyway, and that was Ruby's job again. Sam Bloom, president of Bloom Advertising and chairman of the host committee for Kennedy's visit to Dallas, managed to arrange the opportunity and informed Ruby of the timing, providing him with an alibi as translator for the Yiddish press.

Let's now conclude our overview of the evidence regarding the dual assassinations of the Kennedy brothers. Beside the fact that John and Robert were brothers, their assassinations have at least two things in common: Johnson and Israel.

First, their deaths are precisely framed by Johnson's presidency — also the context for other political assassinations, such as Martin-Luther King's. Johnson became president the very day of John's death, and ended his term a few months after Robert's death, so he was in the position to control both investigations. It has always been a question why Johnson stepped down after Robert announced his candidacy in 1968. The assumption that he didn't believe he could win doesn't fit his character. Rather, he and his sponsors must have calculated that a second Kennedy murdered on Johnson's path to the presidency would be just too hard to push down the throat of the American public.

Secondly, in both cases, we find the fingerprints of Israel's deep state. In the case of Robert, it is the choice of the manipulated patsy, obviously to disguise Robert's assassination as an act of hatred against Israel and give Israel a perfect alibi while stirring anti-Palestinian feelings. In the case of John, it is the identity of the man asked to kill the patsy, a Jewish gangster linked to the Irgun and to the Jewish Murder Inc.

Johnson and Israel, the two common elements in the Kennedy assassinations, are themselves closely linked, since Johnson can be considered as a high-level *sayan,* a man secretly devoted to Israel, or owned by Israel, to the point of committing high treason against the nation he had sworn to protect.

What should have been obvious from the start now appears brightly clear: in order to solve the mystery of the assassination of John Kennedy, one simply had to look into the two other assassinations which are directly connected to it: the assassination of Lee Harvey Oswald, the man whose trial would have exposed the lie and possibly the conspirators; and the assassination of Robert Kennedy, the man who would have reopened the case if he had lived. And both these assassinations bear the signature of Israel.

The causal link between the two assassinations then becomes obvious: even if Robert had been pro-Israel, which he was not, Israel and Johnson would still have had a compelling reason to eliminate him before he got to the White House. Whether he would have gotten to the bottom of it is another matter. RFK probably didn't suspect Israel, and he was surrounded by Jews. He could count on neither his elder brother nor his father to help him (Joe was rendered paralyzed and mute by a stroke in 1961). But the old guard of JFK's Irish friends might have come to help.

CHAPTER 5
Jim Angleton, Mossad's CIA Asset

The "World War III" Virus

Most readers will be at least vaguely familiar with how Lee Harvey Oswald was presented to the public from the day of his alleged shooting of Kennedy, and with some of the anomalies in his background. Here is a brief reminder. In 1959, after being discharged from the U.S. Marine Corps, Oswald had officially renounced his U.S. citizenship and defected to the U.S.S.R. He came back to the U.S. in June 1962 with a Russian wife. In June 1963, he asked for a passport and obtained it overnight, naming the Soviet Union as his destination. On August 9, 1963, Oswald was arrested in New Orleans while passing out Fair Play for Cuba leaflets, and twelve days later got an opportunity to proclaim his Communist convictions in a televised interview.

This background information was made public immediately after Oswald's arrest. The November 23 morning edition of the *Washington Post* carried a front-page story titled, "Pro-Castro Fort Worth Marxist Charged in Kennedy's Assassination."[204] Naturally, Castro smelt "a new trap, an ambush, a Machiavellian plot against our country," as he shared on Cuban television the same day; "on the very blood of their assassinated president there might be unscrupulous people who would begin to work out immediately an aggressive policy against Cuba."[205]

At this point, the public was still unaware of even more incriminating "evidence" that Oswald had acted as a Castro or Soviet agent. Between September 27 and October 1st, 1963, a man identifying himself as Lee Harvey Oswald visited several times both the Cuban Consulate and the Soviet Embassy in Mexico City, applying for immediate visas to both countries while complaining ostentatiously when told about procedures and delays. Besides these visits — monitored by the local CIA station — "Oswald" made an incriminating phone call to the Soviet Embassy, in which he associated himself with a consular official named Vladimir Kostikov, who was known to the FBI as "the officer-in-charge for Western Hemisphere terrorist activities — including and especially assassinations." On October 9, the CIA Station of Mexico City informed CIA headquarters about this wiretapped call from "an American male who spoke broken Russian" and who "said his name was Lee Oswald." I quote directly from James Douglass for the rest of the story:

> On November 18, 1963, the Soviet Embassy in Washington received a crudely typed, badly spelled letter dated nine days earlier and signed by "Lee Harvey Oswald" of Dallas. The timing of the letter's arrival was no accident. Its contents made it a Cold War propaganda bomb whose trigger would be Kennedy's assassination. Read in the context of Dallas four days later, the text of the letter seemed to implicate the Soviet Union in conspiring with Oswald to murder the U.S. president. Three paragraphs in particular laid the blame for the assassination at the door of the Russians. The letter's first paragraph read: "This is to inform you of recent events sincem [*sic*] my meetings with comrade Kostin [a diminutive of Kostikov] in the Embassy of the Soviet Union, Mexico City, Mexico." ... The letter's third paragraph read: "I had not planned to contact the Soviet embassy in Mexico so they were unprepared, had I been able to reach the Soviet embassy in Havana as planned, the embassy there would have had time to complete our business." ... The letter's fourth paragraph states: "Of corse [*sic*] the Soviet embassy was not at fault, they were, as I say unprepared, the Cuban consulate was guilty of a gross breach of regulations, I am glad he has since been replced [*sic*]."

After Kennedy's assassination, on November 26, Soviet ambassador Anatoly Dobrynin sent a "Top Secret/Highest Priority" telegram from Washington to Moscow about this letter, saying "this letter was clearly a provocation." He added that, "The competent U.S. authorities are undoubtedly aware of this letter, since the embassy's correspondence is under constant surveillance," and he recommended that the Soviet government pass it on to U.S. authorities, "because if we don't pass it on, the organizers of this entire provocation could use this fact to try casting suspicion on us." Dobrynin received agreement from Moscow: "You may send [U.S. Secretary of State Dean] Rusk photocopies of the correspondence between the embassy and Oswald."[206]

Meanwhile, it would be determined by the FBI that the voice of the person calling the Soviet Embassy (taped by the Mexico CIA station) didn't fit the real Oswald (who was almost fluent in Russian), and neither did his picture taken at the entry of the Soviet Embassy. Edgar Hoover informed Johnson by phone on November 23: "That picture and the tape do not correspond to this man [the real Oswald]'s voice, nor to his appearance." The real Oswald had never gone to Mexico, and declared so after his arrest. There is therefore little doubt that an Oswald impersonator had been sent to create, under CIA surveillance, a connection between Oswald and a KGB expert in assassination, including preparation to exfiltrate Oswald after an assassination. Oswald, as Douglass writes, "was being systematically set up for his scapegoat role."

There is much more to the story, but these are the key elements that support the theory that proofs of Oswald's motive and premeditation had been fabricated in advance by the CIA. According to the most common version of that theory, the purpose was to blame the Dallas shooting on Cuba and/or the Soviet Union — a classic false flag scenario. Besides getting rid of Kennedy, the theory goes, the motive was to create a pretext for invading Cuba, something that Kennedy had strictly forbidden after the Bay of Pigs debacle and the firing of Allen Dulles. That theory has become so dominant in JFK research that most conspiracy-minded people would consider it as proven beyond doubt. However, it has one major flaw: there was no invasion of Cuba following Kennedy's assassination.

The pretext for invading Cuba was neutralized when Johnson and Hoover, followed by the Warren Commission, proclaimed

Oswald to be a lone nut. According to Douglass, "The CIA's case scapegoated Cuba and the U.S.S.R. through Oswald for the president's assassination and steered the United States toward an invasion of Cuba and a nuclear attack on the U.S.S.R. *However, LBJ did not want to begin his presidency with a global war*" (my emphasis). Johnson, we are told, thwarted the plot of the CIA and Pentagon hawks to start World War III. "To Johnson's credit, he refused to let the Soviets take the blame for Kennedy's murder; to his discredit, he decided not to confront the CIA over what it had done in Mexico City. Thus, while the secondary purpose of the assassination plot was stymied, its primary purpose was achieved." [207] The problem with this theory is its internal contradiction, since it also affirms that the reason Kennedy was assassinated was that he refused to start World War III: therefore, starting the war was the primary — not the secondary — purpose of the whole thing. A bigger problem is that it ignores all the evidence of Johnson's complicity in the Dallas coup, and his own warmongering record.

The alternative explanation is that Oswald's profile as a Communist assassin was crafted by the conspirators, not for the purpose of starting a war against Cuba and Russia, but for allowing Johnson to bully Federal and State administrations into closing the investigation quickly, lest the discovery of Cuba and Russia's responsibility force the U.S. into a global nuclear war "that would kill 40 million Americans in an hour," as Johnson kept repeating to everyone from Dallas to Washington. To convince Senator Richard Russell to sit in the Warren Commission, for example, Johnson told him in a taped phone conversation: "we've go to take this out of the arena where they're testifying that Khrushchev and Castro did this and did that and kicking us into a war that can kill forty million Americans in an hour..." Deputy Attorney General Nicholas Katzenbach — soon to replace Robert Kennedy — produced a memo to press secretary Bill Moyers on November 25, that said:

> The public must be satisfied that Oswald was the assassin; that he did not have confederates who are still at large; and that the evidence was such that he would have been convicted at trial. Speculation about Oswald's motivation ought to be cut off, and we should have some basis for rebutting thought that this was a Communist conspiracy. . .[208]

Besides allowing Johnson to shut down all investigations, the threat of nuclear war kept the American people satisfied that, if they were being lied to — as many felt they were — it was for their own good. And so the lie about Kennedy's assassination was two-sided: on one side was the Cuban-Soviet conspiracy, and on the other was the lone assassin. Both sides of the lie had to be maintained over the years, the Soviet conspiracy remaining in the background in order to keep the Warren Commission's conclusion, if not credible, at least justifiable. That is why, in a September 1969 filmed interview (broadcast on CBS on April 24, 1975), Johnson could calmly declare that "there might have been international connections," but that the Warren Commission did a fine job anyway.[209]

Like most JFK researchers, John Newman, a retired U.S. Army major and Political Science professor, and the author of *Oswald and the CIA*, believes that long before Kennedy's trip to Dallas, Oswald was maneuvered and his activities "carefully monitored, controlled, and, if necessary, embellished and choreographed," so that, "on 22 November, Oswald's CIA files would establish his connection to Castro and the Kremlin." However, in an epilogue added in 2008 to his book, Newman reasons that the real purpose of staging Oswald as a Communist was not to start World War III, but to create a "World War III virus", used by Johnson as a "national security" pretext to shut all investigations. "It is now apparent that the World War III pretext for a national security cover-up was built into the fabric of the plot to assassinate President Kennedy."[210] Peter Dale Scott had come to a similar conclusion in *Deep Politics and the Death of JFK* (1993), where he speaks of a two-phase "dialectical cover-up".[211]

After reviewing the steps taken to design this plot, Newman concludes: "In my view, there is only one person whose hands fit into these gloves: James Jesus Angleton, Chief of CIA's Counterintelligence Staff."

> [W]hoever Oswald's direct handler or handlers were, we must now seriously consider the possibility that Angleton was probably their general manager. No one else in the Agency had the access, the authority, and the diabolically ingenious mind to manage this sophisticated plot. No one else had the means necessary to plant the WWIII virus in Oswald's files and keep it dormant for six weeks until the president's assassination. Whoever those who were ultimately responsible for the decision to kill Kennedy were, their reach extended into the national intelligence apparatus to such a

degree that they could call upon a person who knew its inner secrets and workings so well that he could design a failsafe mechanism into the fabric of the plot. The only person who could ensure a national security cover-up of an apparent counter-intelligence nightmare was the head of counterintelligence.[212]

Newman is not the first Kennedy researcher with an interest in Angleton. His name often comes up in books incriminating the CIA, because he appears as the most likely puppet-master of the patsy Oswald. "In the mid 1970s," writes Douglass, "the Senate's Church Committee on Intelligence and the House Select Committee on Assassinations (HSCA) opened the CIA's lid on Lee Harvey Oswald and discovered James Jesus Angleton." [213]

There is little doubt that the impersonations of Oswald in Mexico City had been engineered by Angleton, and carried out by his Mexico team, which included Winston Scott and David Atlee Phillips.[214] It must be noted that, on May 23, 1963, Angleton had distributed to the Joint Chiefs of Staff and heads of fifteen other U.S. agencies a twenty-seven-page document about Cuban subversive activities. This document, titled "Cuban Control and Action Capabilities," contains the following example of problems to be solved: "An American citizen, for example, can enter Mexico with a tourist card, not even a passport, and obtain a separate visa to Cuba from the Cuban consulate in Mexico City. He can go to Cuba and return supplied with a new tourist card obtained in Cuba without any indication that he has ever been there." Jefferson Morley, who mentions this document, comments: "Angleton was prescient. That is exactly what the defector Lee Oswald would attempt to do four months later. . . . The paper reveals Angleton's personal interest in the Cuban consulate in Mexico City in mid-1963. . . . When the defector Lee Oswald showed up at the Cuban consulate in September 1963, Angleton was not surprised or uninformed. He was prepared."[215]

As I said, the staging of the Communist Oswald linked to a KGB assassin can be interpreted in two opposite ways. For Douglass and other supporters of the CIA theory, this is proof that the conspirators manufactured a pretext to start World War III (but Johnson ruined their plan), whereas for John Newman, the pretext to start World War III was itself the preplanned pretext to close the investigation. I lean strongly toward Newman's interpretation, because there is no evidence of any effort from Angleton, the CIA or the Pentagon to resist Johnson's shut-down order and to exploit the *casus belli.*

In order to make an informed judgment, we need to get acquainted with Angleton's career and profile, using two major biographies of Angleton: Tom Mangold, *Cold Warrior: James Jesus Angleton: The CIA's Master Spy Hunter*, Simon & Schuster, 1991; and Jefferson Morley, *The Ghost: The Secret Life of CIA Spymaster James Jesus Angleton,* St. Martin's Press, 2017.[216]

Angleton and Counterintelligence

During World War II, Angleton served in the counterintelligence branch of the OSS in Milan, where he had grown up. In 1947, he joined the newly created CIA. He was sent back to Italy and played some role in the GLADIO operations that insured the victory of the U.S.-supported Christian Democratic Party over the U.S.S.R.-supported Italian Communist Party. In 1954, the Director of Central Intelligence Allen Dulles appointed Angleton head of the Counterintelligence Staff, a position he kept for twenty years. According to Mangold, "Angleton's longstanding friendships with Dulles and Helms were to become the most important factor in giving him freedom of movement within the CIA. He was extended such trust by his superiors that there was often a significant failure of executive control over his activities."[217]

After Kennedy fired CIA Director Allen Dulles and his two Deputy Directors Richard Bissel and Charles Cabell in autumn 1961, Angleton remained undisturbed. He was totally shielded by CIA Deputy Director Richard Helms. Morley writes: "President Kennedy thought he had reined in the CIA by firing Dulles and Bissell after the Bay of Pigs, but his actions did not much affect Angleton's power. The Counterintelligence chief was now the third-most-powerful man in the CIA and he was accountable to no one."[218] In 1962, as the CIA moved into its new headquarters in Langley, Angleton's Counterintelligence Staff had nearly two hundred people.[219]

As one colleague and friend said, "Jim's central dominating obsession was communism, something that for him was the essence of absolute and profound *evil.* For him nothing else really mattered, but he would use anyone and anything to combat it."[220] The most secret component of Angleton's empire was the Special Investigation Group (SIG), tasked with exploring the possibility that the CIA itself was penetrated by the KGB. "The SIG was so secret that many members of the Counterintelligence Staff didn't even know it existed," write Mangold, "and nearly everyone was denied access to it. . . . Secret units within a secret unit were a hallmark of Angleton, the SIG, and the Counterintelligence Staff."[221]

The tragicomic story of Angleton's "mole hunt" is told in detail by Tom Mangold. It involves a megalomaniac KGB defector named Anatoly Golitsyn, who, responding to Angleton's paranoia, convinced him that the KGB had infiltrated the CIA through a high-level source code-named "Sacha", and that all other defectors after him would be phony. Angleton's quest for Sacha would last seven years and produce no result other than profound damage to the Agency. Anyone who spoke Russian was targeted, and 75 percent of the top Soviet Division officers were removed. At least 22 genuine defectors were turned away, sometimes betrayed to the KGB. Eventually, 40 senior Agency officers were put on the suspect list and many had their careers ruined. All were exonerated and indemnified later. No real KGB spy was ever caught by Angleton. The irony of it all is that one Counterintelligence agent tasked to find "Sacha", Clare Edward Petty, ended up believing it was Angleton himself.[222] This fiasco is the subject of David C. Martin's book *Wilderness of Mirrors: Intrigue, Deception, and the Secrets that Destroyed Two of the Cold War's Most Important Agents* (2018). Martin summarizes the paranoid mentality that Angleton infused into the CIA: "A man's successes could be used against him by suggesting that he must have had help from the other side, while his failures could be brought forward as evidence of deliberately destructive behavior."[223]

When William Colby, after heading the Soviet Division, became Director of the CIA, he looked for a pretext to sack Angleton. "I couldn't find that we ever caught a spy under Jim," he later told Mangold and other journalists like David Wise, who concludes: "In the end, Angleton never found a mole. But he did more harm to the CIA than even the most talented mole could ever have accomplished."[224] In December 1974, Colby fired Angleton after the disclosure by Seymour Hersh in the *New York Times* of two dubious domestic operations that his Counterintelligence Staff had been conducting in violation of the CIA's charter: intercepting mail sent between the United States and the Soviet Union

(Program HT/LINGUAL) and spying on American antiwar protestors (Operation CHAOS).

When George Kalaris, who replaced Angleton, directed an investigation into Angleton's files, his team identified over 40 vaults that had to be drilled open. It took three years to sort and classify the discovered materials, which had never been archived into the CIA's central filing system. And it took CIA officer Cleveland Cram six years to write a report in 12 legal-sized volumes on the activities of the Counterintelligence Staff from 1954 to 1974, "a story of madness that the CIA prefers to keep hidden, even 40 years later," says Morley.[225]

The obvious conclusion is that Angleton's Counterintelligence, which was involved in the preparation for JFK's assassination, was not the CIA, but rather a kind of alternative CIA, a "second CIA within the CIA" as Peter Dale Scott puts it, sealed from scrutiny and accountable to no one, yet supported by almost unlimited budget.[226] During Kennedy's presidency, John McCone, an outsider, of course had no idea what Angleton was doing or not doing, and Richard Helms, his Deputy, "let Angleton do as he pleased, few questions asked," Morley writes. "From this position, [Angleton] built an empire, his own clandestine service housed within the CIA."[227]

But this Counterintelligence disaster is only half of Angleton's story. There is another half, rarely told. Tom Mangold only refers to it in an endnote, to shield himself from the accusation of self-censorship:

> I would like to place on the record, however, that Angleton's professional friends overseas, then and subsequently, came from the Mossad (the Israeli intelligence-gathering service) and that he was held in immense esteem by his Israeli colleagues and by the state of Israel, which was to award him profound honors after his death.[228]

To be fair, Mangold also writes: "Angleton's ties with the Israelis gave him considerable prestige within the CIA and later added significantly to his expanding counterintelligence empire," while stirring "the utter fury of the division's separate Arab desks."[229] But that's all we'll learn from Mangold about the Mossad side of Angleton. To know more about it, we must turn to Jefferson Morley's more recent and thorough investigation. We will learn that Angleton's Mossad friends were not just "overseas", but ubiquitous in Washington and Langley, and that Angleton was

less "out of control" than we think — only the people who
controlled him were not those who were supposed to.

Angleton and Mossad

When Angleton became chief of Counterintelligence in 1954,
he had already been occupying, since early 1951, the CIA's Israeli
Desk, or Israeli Account, as it was called. And he had already
exclusive authority on the CIA station in Tel Aviv. The Israeli
Desk was created for Angleton after the visit of Prime Minister
David Ben-Gurion to the United States in May 1951. Besides
launching a drive to raise $1 billion from the sale of Israel
Bonds,[230] the purpose of Ben-Gurion's visit was to establish a
collaboration between U.S. and Israeli intelligence agencies.
Israel's population of immigrants from the U.S.S.R. and Eastern
Europe made the country a privileged source of information about
what was going on behind the Iron Curtain. In exchange for this
service, Israel wanted strategic, economic and military support
against their enemy Nasser, whom they did their utmost to push
into the Soviet camp. Here is Morley's account of the background
for that turning point in U.S.-Israel relationship:

> In 1950, Reuven Shiloah, the founder of Israel's first intelligence
> organization, visited Washington and came away impressed by the
> CIA. In April 1951, he reorganized the fractious Israeli security
> forces to create a new foreign intelligence agency, called the
> Institute for Intelligence and Special Tasks, inevitably known as
> the Mossad, the Hebrew word for "institute." In 1951, Prime
> Minister David Ben-Gurion came to the United States and brought
> Shiloah with him. Ben-Gurion met privately with President
> Truman and Walter Bedell Smith [director of CIA]. Angleton
> arranged for Ben-Gurion to lunch with Allen Dulles [Deputy
> Director for Plans]. . . . Shiloah stayed on in Washington to work
> out the arrangements with Angleton. The resulting agreement laid
> the foundation for the exchange of secret information between the
> two services and committed them to report to each other on
> subjects of mutual interest. Shiloah, according to his biographer
> [Haggai Eshed], soon developed "a special relationship" with
> Angleton, who became the CIA's exclusive liaison with the
> Mossad. Angleton returned the favor by visiting Israel. Shiloah
> introduced him to Amos Manor, chief of counterespionage for
> Israel's domestic intelligence agency [1953-1963], known as
> Shabak or Shin Bet.[231]

For almost 25 years, Angleton was the CIA's exclusive liaison with Israeli intelligence. In this capacity, recalled one of his friends interviewed by Andrew and Leslie Cockburn for their book *Dangerous Liaison: The Inside Story of the U.S.-Israeli Covert Relationship*, "he was getting the benefit of Israeli networks and connections all over the place, not just in the Communist bloc."[232]

Angleton's special channel to the Mossad didn't profit much the U.S. in terms of "intelligence". In October 1956, no warning came from Angleton about the Israelis' plan to invade Egypt. As rumors of war were reaching the State Department, Robert Amory, head of the CIA Directorate of Intelligence, called an emergency meeting on October 26. After he presented Allen Dulles with evidence that the Israelis "were mobilizing to attack someone — Egypt," Angleton contradicted him saying, "I can discount what Amory is saying. I spent last night with our friends and they have assured me that they are just carrying out protective measures against the Jordanians." Amory got mad and said to Dulles: "The taxpayer lays out $16,000 a year to me as your deputy director for me to give you the best intelligence available. Either you believe me or you believe this co-opted Israeli agent here [pointing to Angleton]."[233] Within days, Israel had invaded Egypt's Sinai.

James Jesus Angleton made his first visit to Israel in October 1951. "By the mid-1950s," Morley writes, "Angleton liked nothing better than to leave the cramped office politics of Washington for the austere frontier of the Holy Land. On his visits, Angleton stayed in Ramat Gan, on the suburban coastal plain north of Tel Aviv, the home to many Israeli intelligence officers and diplomats."

> "He used to come from time to time, to meet the head of Mossad, to get briefings," recalls Efraim Halevy, who served as the Mossad's liaison officer to the CIA station in Tel Aviv in the early 1960s. Halevy escorted Angleton on his rounds and recorded his meetings with Israeli officials. "He used to meet with David Ben-Gurion, whom he knew for many years," Halevy recalled. "Ben-Gurion ultimately left office [in 1963] and Angleton went down to Sde Boker [Ben-Gurion's home in the Negev] to meet him. I didn't attend those meetings. Those were just the two of them. He had business to transact."[234]

Angleton knew at least six of the men closest to Ben-Gurion and privy to his secrets. Besides Efraim Halevy (on the left in this chapter's head picture), he befriended Isser Harel, founder of the

Shin Bet and chief of the Mossad from 1951 ("Jim had enormous admiration for Isser," said Halevy). Angleton also enjoyed the lifetime friendship of Amos Manor, director of Shin Bet from 1953 to 1963, of Teddy Kollek, who later became mayor of Jerusalem, and of Meir Amit, head of Mossad from 1963 to 1968. When Halevy accompanied Yitzhak Rabin for his ambassadorship to Washington (1968-1973), Angleton met him as often as five times a week, and had monthly lunches with Rabin, Halevy recalled. Angleton's friends were among the builders of the Zionist state, and Angleton was the only American authorized to talk to them.[235]

This, coupled with his infatuation with Zionism, gave Angleton a great influence on Washington's Israeli policy. According to Morley, "he was a leading architect of America's strategic relationship with Israel that endures and dominates the region to this day." [236] "Angleton's influence on U.S.-Israeli relations between 1951 and 1974 exceeded that of any secretary of state, with the possible exception of Henry Kissinger. His influence was largely unseen by Congress, the press, other democratic institutions, and much of the CIA itself."[237]

Dimona and the Stolen Uranium

Naturally, Angleton's influence on U.S.-Israeli relationship touched upon the sensitive question of Israel's military nuclear ambition. Morley again:

> In Washington, he and Cicely [Angleton's wife] had spent many evenings with Memi de Shalit, a Lithuanian-born military intelligence officer stationed in the Israeli embassy. Angleton "adored" de Shalit and his wife, Ada, said Efraim Halevy. The de Shalits moved back to Israel in the 1950s, but the friendship continued, and it brought Angleton into the circle of other knowledgeable Israelis. Amos de Shalit, Memi's brother, was a professor of nuclear physics at the Weizmann Institute of Science in Tel Aviv. He would be a major contributor to the Israeli nuclear program.[238]

According to Seymour Hersh, "Angleton's close personal ties with the DeShalit family and others in Israel made it inevitable that he would learn about the [Dimona] construction in the Negev." Yet he never reported on the Israelis' efforts to build a nuclear reactor for military purposes.[239] In 1960, Angleton ignored a request from the U.S. Intelligent Board, which reviewed CIA operations on behalf of the White House, that all information regarding Dimona be transmitted "expeditiously".[240]

Angleton also failed to notice, or to report, about the stealing of weapons-grade enriched uranium from a plant of the Nuclear Materials and Equipment Corporation (NUMEC) in Apollo, Pennsylvania. The NUMEC had been created under U.S. government license by David Lowenthal, a Zionist financier, and was run by Zalman Shapiro, the son of an Orthodox rabbi from Lithuania, who was also head of the local chapter of the Zionist Organization of America. Over the 9 years from 1959 to 1968, the Atomic Energy Commission estimated that 267 kilograms of uranium went missing at the Apollo NUMEC plant. One Israeli masquerading as a nuclear engineer who visited the plant was a Mossad agent named Rafael Eitan, who was known to Angleton. "With the fissile material diverted from NUMEC, Israel was able to construct its first nuclear weapon by 1967 and become a full-blown nuclear power by 1970 — the first, and still the only, nuclear power in the Middle East. Angleton, it is fair to say, thought collaboration with Israel was more important than U.S. non-proliferation policy."[241]

"Angleton's loyalty to Israel betrayed U.S. policy on an epic scale," Morley concludes. "Instead of supporting U.S. nuclear security policy, he ignored it." John Hadden, then CIA station chief in Tel Aviv, who felt betrayed by his superior Angleton, wrote in 1978, "A crime was committed 10 or 20 years ago, a crime considered so serious that for its commission the death penalty is mandatory and no statute of limitations applies."

> Angleton had regular professional and personal contact with at least six men aware of Israel's secret plan to build a bomb. From Asher Ben-Natan to Amos de Shalit to Isser Harel to Meir Amit to Moshe Dayan to Yval Ne'eman, his friends were involved in the building of Israel's nuclear arsenal. If he learned anything of the secret program at Dimona, he reported very little of it. . . . The failure of the U.S. nonproliferation policy to prevent the introduction of nuclear weapons to the Middle East in the 1960s is part of Angleton's legacy, and its effects will be felt for decades, if not centuries.[242]

Angleton himself implicitly acknowledged his role to *New York Times* foreign correspondent Tad Szulc, who declared before the Church Committee in 1975:

I was told by one of my news sources that a situation had occurred in the 1960s in which the CIA delivered to the Israeli government classified information, technical knowledge, know-how, the services of distinguished physicists and fissionable material in the form of plutonium to assist in the development of an Israeli nuclear weapon at the Dimona Israeli Nuclear Testing grounds. . . I have raised the subject in a private conversation with Mr. James Angleton in the spring of this year [April 1975]. Mr. Angleton told me that essentially this information was correct.[243]

The Six Day War and the USS Liberty

According to Andrew and Leslie Cockburn, "There is a body of opinion within the American intelligence community that Angleton played a leading part in orchestrating the events leading up to the June 1967 war. One long-serving official at CIA's ancient rival, the code-breaking National Security Agency, states flatly that 'Jim Angleton and the Israelis spent a year cooking up the '67 war. It was a CIA operation designed to get Nasser.'"[244]

In this period, according to Joan Mellen, author of *Blood in the Water: How the US and Israel Conspire to Ambush the USS Liberty* (2018), "Meir Amit was Angleton's chief ally in Israel, but in the United States, he relied on another Mossad operative, Ephraim 'Eppy' Evron, who in 1967, as a Mossad operative as well as deputy Israeli ambassador to Washington, enjoyed greater importance at the Israeli embassy than the ambassador, Avraham Harman. It was Evron who had arranged meetings between Angleton and Moshe Dayan . . . to discuss the feasibility of an attack on Egypt with the objective of toppling Nasser. Lyndon Johnson had authorized Angleton to inform Evron that the United States would not intervene to stop an attack on Egypt."[245]

In May 1967, Eppy Evron met Johnson at the White House. Evron later said that Johnson told him, "You and I are going to pass another Tonkin resolution," in reference to the mock incident in the Gulf of Tonkin that Johnson used to justify the aggression against North Vietnam.[246] On May 30, Meir Amit, then head of global operations for Mossad, flew to Washington and met first with Angleton the next day. There is no documentary record of their conversation, but on June 1, Amit reported to Israel: "there is a growing chance for American political backing if we act on our own."[247] "It would be Angleton," says Mellen, "who would prevail in formulating, with Meir Amit, the configuration of the operation that would culminate in the attack on the USS *Liberty*."[248]

Here a summary of Tom Segev's account of this meeting in *1967: Israel, the War, and the Year That Transformed the Middle East* (2007): "Amit's trip to Washington had ben instigated by Aharon Yariv, and its main purpose was to find out, through intelligence channels, what the Americans would really do if Israel attacked Egypt." The first person Amit met there was James Jesus Angleton, who introduced him to Helms, head of CIA. Helms "arranged for Amit to meet with Secretary of Defense McNamara." Presenting Israel's plan to attack Egypt, Amit "heard no objections from McNamara." McNamara was called out of the meeting twice to talk with Johnson on the phone, and reported to Amit the President's message: "I read you loud and clear." Amit reported back to Israel his impression that the Americans would give their blessing to an Israeli strike "crushing Nasser." In response to Eshkol's question, Amit said they might even assist Israel in such a strike. "Jim Angleton was enthusiastic," writes Segev; he saw in Israel's strike "the possibility of solving the region's problems." He "stressed the issue's delicacy and asked to preserve complete secrecy." When corresponding with Eshkol on the phone, Amit acknowledged the decisive importance of Angleton's support. Angleton, he said, intimated that the Americans "would undoubtedly look positively on a knockout" on Egypt; "Angleton was an extraordinary asset for us. We could not have found ourselves a better advocate." He was "the biggest Zionist of the lot," insisted Amit.[249]

In December 1967, having doubled their territory, the Israelis threw a big party for Angleton when he visited them on his 50th birthday.

Conclusion

The Mossad side of Angleton is part of the unspoken Kennedy truth. It is no small part. As Morley writes, "Angleton's formative and sometimes decisive influence on U.S. policy toward Israel can be seen in many areas — from the impotence of U.S. nuclear non-proliferation policy in the region, to Israel's triumph in the 1967 Six-Day War, to the feeble U.S. response to the attack on the *Liberty*, to the intelligence failure represented by the Yom Kippur War of 1973."[250]

Angleton is remembered in the U.S. as a mentally insane man who caused irreparable damage to the CIA's efficiency and reputation. In contrast, he is remembered in Israel as a great benefactor of the Zionist state. Here is an extract from the *Washington Post* report about a ceremony held in his honor in Jerusalem after his death. Although it was supposedly secret, a couple of Israeli reporters, including Andy Court of the *Jerusalem Post,* had been tipped off and attended:

The head of the pathologically secretive spy agency, the Mossad, was there, as was his counterpart with Shin Bet, the Israeli internal security service. Five former heads of those agencies and three former military intelligence chiefs were also present. Their mission: to pay final tribute to a beloved member of their covert fraternity — the late CIA chief of counterintelligence, James Jesus Angleton. . . . Following the planting [of trees], the group gathered again in Jerusalem behind the King David Hotel at a scenic spot not far from the walls of the Old City that Angleton often visited on his trips here. There they dedicated a memorial stone that read, in English, Hebrew and Arabic: "In memory of a dear friend, James (Jim) Angleton." . . . The ceremonies symbolized the respect and affection that the Israeli intelligence community holds for Angleton . . . Although his name appears in few history books about Israel, Angleton played a crucial role in the early years of the young Jewish state. In the 1950s and early 1960s, when most of official Washington was wary of — even hostile to — Israel, he helped forge links between the Mossad and the CIA that established the basis for cooperation in intelligence gathering that still exists today. . . . Angleton "was a friend you could trust on a personal basis," said Defense Minister Yitzhak Rabin, who spoke at the tree-planting ceremony. Rabin knew Angleton from his days as Israeli Army chief of staff in the mid-1960s and later as ambassador to the United States. Jerusalem Mayor Teddy Kollek, who rose from his sickbed to attend the ceremonies, told the small crowd, "We commemorate a great friend, who saw Israel-U.S. relations through their most difficult period in the 40 years of Israel's existence." . . . Those who attended, according to Court, included the current heads of the Mossad and Shin Bet, neither of whom can be named under government security laws; former Mossad chiefs Meir Amit, Zvi Zamir and Yitzhak Hofi; former Shin Bet chiefs Avraham Ahituv and Amos Manor, and former military intelligence heads Aharon Yariv, Shlomo Gazit and Binyamin Gibli.[251]

There is still a mystery about Angleton's relationship with Israel, a mystery that perhaps Angleton himself could not have cleared up. It is a reasonable guess that most of Angleton's Israeli friends were well aware of his personality issues and of his delusional worldview, and that they exploited them to the fullest; they convinced Angleton, for example, that they were his indispensable allies against Communism. One former Mossad chief said to the Cockburns: "Of course, Jim had some pretty weird ideas, like that one about the Sino-Soviet split [Angleton believed it was a cunning deception]. But I think that he found himself a little more appreciated here in Israel than in Washington. We would listen respectfully to him [here the smirk] and his opinions." The Israelis, gather the Cockburns, "took great care to flatter him and bend a respectful ear to his interpretation of events in the shadowy world of intelligence and deception." Taking a closer look at the Angleton memorial in the Jerusalem forest, the Cockburns point out that, "Unlike the other memorial groves, the inscription here is not carved in stone, but is written on a sheet of plastic screwed to the stone itself. Within a year of the commemoration of the site most of the trees, tiny saplings, were dead or dying. The ground all around was covered in garbage: cans, rags, and, here and there, bones."[252] What kind of memorial is this? A memorial for a useful idiot that needs not be remembered too long?

What was Angleton's position in the organizational chart of John Kennedy's assassination? If, as John Newman and many others believe, Angleton was the "general manager" of Oswald's handlers, and the engineer of his mock appearance in Mexico, what did he really know of Oswald's ultimate function in the plot? There is no indication that Angleton ever felt that he had been used by his Israeli friends, and it is therefore more than likely that he was a deliberate and key participant in the conspiracy to kill Kennedy. What has been shown beyond a reasonable doubt, at any rate, is that Angleton, the central CIA player in the plot, was in reality more controlled by the Mossad than by the CIA itself.

CHAPTER 6
Joe, the Cursed Peacemaker

"Joseph P. Kennedy," writes Laurence Leamer, "created one great thing in his life, and that was his family. . . . Joe taught that blood ruled and that they must trust each other and venture out into a dangerous world full of betrayals and uncertainty, always returning to the sanctuary of family."[253]

I have emphasized already that, although very different in character, John and Robert may be seen, for their historical significance, as essentially one person killed twice. But it must be stressed that the source of their brotherly bond was filial piety. This is clear from the way Robert became John's Attorney General, as told by historian David Nasaw in his biography, *The Patriarch: The Remarkable Life and Turbulent Times of Joseph P. Kennedy* (2012). It was Joe who insisted that Robert be given this position. Robert initially refused, arguing that "nepotism was a problem." John was reluctant to pressure Bobby, but "Joseph Kennedy refused to budge," and explained to them "why Jack needed someone in the cabinet in whom he had complete and

absolute trust. The Kennedys would always be outsiders, unable to
fully trust anyone but family members. Jack needed all the
protection he could get." Still, John wouldn't yield.

> He decided to offer Bobby the number two position at the Defense
> Department and asked Clark Clifford, who was running his
> transition team, to go to New York to explain to [Joe] Kennedy,
> who had flown there after visiting Jackie and his new grandson in
> the hospital, why Bobby should not be named attorney general.
> Clifford agreed, though he thought it rather odd that the president-
> elect had asked "a third party to try to talk to his father about his
> brother." Clifford met Kennedy at Kennedy's apartment and
> presented his carefully rehearsed case against the appointment. "I
> was pleased with my presentation; it was, I thought, persuasive.
> When I had finished, Kennedy said, 'Thank you very much, Clark.
> I am so glad to have heard your views.' Then, pausing a moment,
> he said, 'I do want to leave you with one thought, however — one
> firm thought.' He paused again, and looked me straight in the eye.
> *'Bobby is going to be Attorney General.* All of us have worked our
> tails off for Jack, and now that we have succeeded I am going to
> see to it that Bobby gets the same chance that we gave to Jack.' I
> would always," Clifford recalled years later, "remember the
> intense but matter-of-fact tone with which he had spoken — there
> was no rancor, no anger, no challenge." The father had spoken,
> and his sons, on this issue at least, were expected to obey.[254]

Although there is no recorded statement to that effect, Joe
probably envisioned that Robert could succeed Jack as president in
1968. And it is easy to imagine that, had John survived and been
reelected in 1964, Robert, with John's support, could have
succeeded him (under his watch). We may ponder what the world
would be like today had there been Kennedys in the White House
until 1976.

The stain of appeasement

There can be no understanding of the Kennedy brothers
without some understanding of their father, Joseph Patrick
Kennedy, for this is where they came from, not only in their own
eyes and those of their friends, but in the eyes of their enemies too.

As everyone knows, while Joe Kennedy served as U.S.
ambassador to London, he was one of the most outspoken
supporters of Neville Chamberlain's policy of appeasement in
1938-39, and for this he ended in the wrong side of history. That
is, of course, because standard historiography of WWII follows

what may be called the Churchillian perspective — since Churchill was its earliest and most influential creator ("History will be kind to me, for I intend to write it").[255]

But in examining Joe's career, it is important to remember that Chamberlain's return from Munich on 30 September 1938, and his subsequent "Peace for our time" speech, were greeted by almost universal euphoria. The point was made by A. J. P. Taylor in *The Origins of the Second World War* (1961):

> Historians do a bad day's work when they write the appeasers off as stupid or as cowards. They were men confronted with real problems, doing their best in the circumstances of their time. They recognized that an independent and powerful Germany had somehow to be fitted into Europe. Later experience suggests that they were right. . . . the "appeasers" feared that the defeat of Germany would be followed by a Russian domination over much of Europe. Later experience suggests that they were right here also. . . . Nor is it true that the "appeasers" were a narrow circle, widely opposed at the time. . . . On the contrary, few causes have been more popular. Every newspaper in the country applauded the Munich settlement with the exception of *Reynold's News*.[256]

Appeasers were peacemakers. "I am pro-peace, I pray, hope, and work for peace," Joe declared on his first return from London to the U.S. in December 1938.[257]

That could have been his son's motto too. President Kennedy was also a determined peacemaker, and those in the Pentagon who wanted to push the U.S. into a third world war tried to destabilize him with insinuations that he was an appeaser like his father. On October 19, 1962, in the heat of the Cuban Missile Crisis, as Kennedy resolved to blockade Soviet shipments rather than bomb and invade Cuba, General Curtis LeMay scornfully told him, "This is almost as bad as the appeasement at Munich . . . I just don't see any other solution except direct military intervention *right now*."[258]

The stain of his father's record as an Hitler-appeaser had followed John like a shadow. Although the press had not published it, it was no secret in the Pentagon and the CIA that the U.S. army had discovered in 1946, in Berlin's Foreign Office, reports about Joe's meetings with German ambassador von Ribbentrop and his successor von Dirksen, that said that Joe was Germany's "best friend" in London and "understood our Jewish policy comple-tely."[259] That was a sore spot for the Kennedys. In a joint debate during the 1960 Democratic convention, Johnson had attacked John as being the son of a "Chamberlain umbrella man" who "thought Hitler was right." [260] During Kennedy's presidential campaign, the Israeli press worried that Kennedy's father "never loved the Jews and therefore there is a question about whether the father did not inject some poisonous drops of anti-Semitism in the minds of his children, including his son John's." [261] Abraham Feinberg recalls that when he invited Kennedy to his apartment to discuss his campaign funding with "all the leading Jews," one of them set the tone with this remark: "Jack, everybody knows the reputation of your father concerning Jews and Hitler. And everybody knows that the apple doesn't fall far from the tree." Kennedy came back outraged from that meeting (but with the promise of $500,000). [262] When meeting the new president on May 30, 1961 in New York, Ben-Gurion could not help but see in him the son of a Hitler-appeaser. Feinberg (who arranged the meeting) recalls that "Ben-Gurion could be vicious, and he had such a hatred of the old man [Joe Kennedy]." [263]

Is Joe's bad reputation among Jews relevant to the assassination of his two sons? Many Jewish authors think it is. In his book *The Kennedy Curse,* purporting to explain "why tragedy has haunted America's first family for 150 years", Edward Klein links the "Kennedy curse" to Joe's anti-Semitism, citing a story "told in mystical Jewish circles" (perhaps made up by Klein) according to which, in "retaliation" to some remark Joe made to "Israel Jacobson, a poor Lubavitcher rabbi and six of his yeshiva students, who were fleeing the Nazis," "Rabbi Jacobson put a curse on Kennedy, damning him and all his male offspring to tragic fates." [264] Ronald Kessler, for his part, wrote a book titled, *The Sins of the Father* — a not so subtle allusion to Exodus 20:5: "I, Yahweh, am a jealous God, punishing the children for the sin of the parents to the third and fourth generation of those who hate me." Naturally, for Kessler, Joe Kennedy's worst sin was that "he was a documented anti-Semite and an appeaser of Adolf Hitler" who "admired the Nazis." [265]

The "Kennedy curse" did run into the third generation and possibly the fourth, when John's only son died in a suspicious plane accident on July 16, 1999, with his wife, possibly pregnant. Five days later, John Podhoretz, son of neoconservative luminary Norman Podhoretz, published in the *New York Post* an opinion piece titled "A Conversation in Hell" in which he imagined Satan speaking to Joe Kennedy in Hell. The devil rejoices at the idea of eternally torturing Joe for "saying all those nice things about

Hitler," and brags of having caused the death of his grandson because, he says: "When I make a deal for a soul like yours, I need to season it before I'm ready to put it in the infernal oven." This hateful fantasy, reminding of the Talmud's depiction of Jesus in Hell, perfectly illustrates the devouring hatred of some Jewish intellectuals toward the Kennedys, and the root of that hatred in Joe Kennedy's effort to prevent the Second World War.[266]

Interestingly, Podhoretz's devil (or is it Yahweh?) accuses Kennedy of having done "everything you could to prevent Jewish emigration from Nazi Germany. Thousands of Jews died because of you."

The truth is exactly the opposite. In 1938, the "Kennedy Plan", as it was called by the press, was to rescue German Jews. Since the U.S. government refused to open its borders to Jewish refugees, and since Great Britain strictly limited Jewish immigration to Palestine, Joe was urging the British government to open up its African colonies for temporary resettlement. "To facilitate the resettlement process," Nasaw writes, "Kennedy volunteered to Halifax that he 'thought that private sources in America might well contribute $100 or $200 million if any large scheme of land settlement could be proposed.'"[267] The plan was presented to Chamberlain just days after *Kristallnacht* (9-10 November 1938), and was supported by Jewish financier Bernard Baruch. But it angered the Zionists, who didn't want to hear about any Jewish emigration except to Palestine, because, Ben-Gurion said, it "will endanger the existence of Zionism."[268] Therefore, today, the "Kennedy Plan" is reviled as a kind of "final solution to the Jewish question," and further proof that Joe was Israel's mortal enemy.[269]

If Jewish hatred of Joe Kennedy could still inspire Podhoretz's nasty column in 1999, imagine how deep it ran in the 1960s. At the height of his showdown with JFK over Dimona, 25 April 1963, Ben-Gurion wrote him a seven-page letter explaining that his people was threatened with extermination by an Arab Federation, just like when "six million Jews in all the countries under Nazi occupations (except Bulgaria), men and women, old and young, infants and babies, were burnt, strangled, buried alive." "Imbued with the lessons of the Holocaust," Avner Cohen comments, "Ben Gurion was consumed by fears for Israel's security."[270] He was enraged by what he saw as Kennedy's obvious lack of concern for his people's security, and at this point, he must have decided that Kennedy was indeed his father's son.

Before we get to the main piece of evidence of a direct relationship between John Kennedy's assassination and his father's legacy, it is necessary to get an overview of Joe's public career. It will also provide an original perspective on the years leading to World War II, which Joe desperately tried to prevent.

DAILY BEAST

Joe Kennedy's Answer to the 'Jewish Question': Ship Them to Africa

| UNDIPLOMATIC |

This week marked the anniversaries of the beginning of the end of the Holocaust and Churchill's death. America's ambassador to Britain, JFK's father, was on the wrong side of both.

Clive Irving   Updated Apr. 14, 2017 12:98PM ET / Published Feb. 01, 2015 6:45AM ET   f y ✉ 👍

The Ambassador

Joe Kennedy entered national politics as a supporter of Roosevelt in his first presidential campaign in 1932. In July 1934, Roosevelt asked him to chair the newly created Securities and Exchange Commission, charged with bringing the New Deal to Wall Street by regulating and disciplining the Stock Exchange market. Kennedy announced: "the days of stock manipulation are over. Things that seemed all right a few years ago find no place in our present-day philosophy." According to Michael Beschloss, author of *Kennedy and Roosevelt: The Uneasy Alliance* (1979), Kennedy "won almost universal praise for his salesmanship, political acumen, and ability to moderate conflicting sides that encouraged capital investment and economic recovery." "Few were more impressed by Kennedy's accomplishment than the man who hired him," and "Joseph Kennedy increasingly became a familiar figure at the White House."[271]

In 1936, Joe supported Roosevelt's second campaign with a book titled *I'm for Roosevelt* (mostly ghost-written by Arthur Krock). He was hoping to be named Secretary of the Treasury, but Henry Morgenthau Jr. also wanted the job, and got it. Instead, Roosevelt named Joe chairman of the Maritime Commission, and one year later made him ambassador to London. As war was brooding in Europe, this was an important position, and Joe made it more important by often overstepping his mandate and his Secretary of State Cordell Hull's instructions.

He supported Chamberlain's position that the territorial integrity of Czechoslovakia was not worth a war, declaring in September 2, 1938, "for the life of me I cannot see anything involved which could be remotely considered worth shedding blood for," for which he was reprimanded by Hull and Roosevelt.[272] On October 19, Joe began another speech by jokingly listing the topics he had decided *not* to talk about, including "a theory of mine that it is unproductive for both democratic and dictator countries to widen the division now existing between them by emphasizing their differences, which are self-apparent."[273] Hull held a press conference the next morning to clarify that Kennedy had been speaking for himself, not the government, and Roosevelt delivered his own display of belligerence: "There can be no peace if national policy adopts as a deliberate instrument the threat of war."[274]

In the meantime, without informing Hull, Kennedy had summoned Charles Lindbergh to London and asked him to write a letter, to be forwarded to Washington and to Whitehall, summarizing his view regarding the strength of the Luftwaffe. Lindbergh had just visited German airfields and installations (and been presented the Service Cross of the German Eagle by Goering), and concluded that the Luftwaffe would be unassailable in a war of the skies. Kennedy then arranged a meeting between Lindbergh and an official of the British air ministry.[275] His diplomatic strategy consisted in trying to convince the British that Germany was unbeatable and that the U.S. wouldn't join the fight, so that the British had better come to terms with Germany, whose territorial claims were justified anyway.

In the same period, Joe made plans to meet in Paris with Dr. Helmuth Wohlthat, Goering's chief economic adviser, with whom he had made contact through James Mooney, the president of General Motors Overseas. As Nasaw explains, "Kennedy was in effect laying the groundwork for a new appeasement strategy, one that would buy Hitler off by providing him with the means to convert his war economy to a peace economy."[276] Hull forbade him to go to Paris, so Joe met Wohlthat in London without informing Hull.

In August 23, 1939, a week before Hitler invaded Poland, Kennedy urged Roosevelt to pressure the Polish government to cede territory to Germany. Roosevelt ignored him.[277] After Hitler's invasion of Poland, Kennedy, like Chamberlain, was heartbroken: "It's the end of the world . . . the end of everything," he told Roosevelt on the phone.[278] But a week later, he was still urging him to save peace, writing him: "It seems to me that this situation may crystallize to a point where the President can be the savior of the world. The British government as such certainly cannot accept any agreement with Hitler, but there may be a point when the President himself may work out plans for world peace."[279]

He got his response from Hull: "The people of the United States would not support any move for peace initiated by this Government that would consolidate or make possible a survival of a regime of force and of aggression." Even before declaring war, the U.S. had adopted the doctrine of unconditional surrender.

Simultaneously, Roosevelt was initiating direct contact with Churchill, now First Lord of the Admiralty and soon to be Prime Minister. Roosevelt's letters gave Churchill enough confidence that the U.S. would ultimately join the war if it broke out. Joe was infuriated when learning about this most irregular channel of communication, at a time when the President was bound by neutrality laws and the American people overwhelmingly opposed to U.S. engagement. Joe was particularly distressed by Roosevelt's trust in Churchill, whom Joe considered "an actor and a politician. He always impressed me that he'd blow up the American Embassy and say it was the Germans if it would get the U.S. in."[280] In early December, 1939, Kennedy confided to Jay Pierrepont Moffat of the State Department that Churchill "is ruthless and scheming. He is also in touch with groups in America which have the same idea, notably, certain strong Jewish leaders."[281]

After the defeat of France, Kennedy saw a new opportunity for peace. He cabled Washington on May 27, 1940, recommending that the President push Britain and France to negotiate an end to the crisis, as Lord Halifax, still Foreign Secretary, was actually proposing. "Only a miracle can save the British expeditionary force from being wiped out or . . . surrender," he wrote. "I suspect that the Germans would be willing to make peace with both the French and British now — of course on their own terms, but on terms that would be a great deal better than they would be if the war continues."[282]

Although aware that Roosevelt was now ignoring him, Joe remained at his post until October 1940. Before leaving, he wrote a note to Chamberlain, then a broken and dying man: "For me to have been any service to you in your struggle is the real worthwhile epoch in my career. You have retired but mark my words the world will yet see that your struggle was never in vain. My job from now on is to tell the world of your hopes. Now and forever, Your devoted friend, Joe Kennedy."[283] Joe Kennedy was still a convinced appeaser, determined to give peace every chance.

David Irving mentions that, before boarding a ship from Lisbon to New York, Kennedy "pleaded with the State Department to announce that, even if this vessel mysteriously blew up in mid-Atlantic with an American ambassador on board, Washington would not consider it a cause for war. 'I thought,' wrote Kennedy in his scurrilous unpublished memoirs, 'that would give me some protection against Churchill's placing a bomb on the ship.'"[284]

Kennedy arrived in New York October 27, a week before election day. He knew enough of Roosevelt's secret contacts with Churchill to endanger his reelection. He was seriously considering speaking out to the press. In a wire to his lover Clare Booth Luce, he promised a bombshell that would "put twenty-five million Catholic voters behind [Republican candidate] Wendell Willkie to throw Roosevelt out."[285]

But Joe had a strong sense of loyalty, and his wife reminded him of a political truth instinctive to them both: "The President sent you, a Roman Catholic, as Ambassador to London, which probably no other President would have done. . . . You would write yourself down as an ingrate in the view of many people if you resign now."[286] After a long conversation with Roosevelt on the day of his arrival, of which nothing transpired, Kennedy gave a radio address over CBS on October 29 to endorse Roosevelt, but not without reasserting his "conviction that this country must and will stay out of war." A few days later, with Joe Kennedy by his side, Roosevelt made his own pledge: "I have said this before, but I shall say it again and again and again: Your boys are not going to be sent into any foreign wars!"[287]

Roosevelt was elected. On December 1, 1940, Kennedy delivered his resignation letter, and told reporters: "My plan is . . . to devote my efforts to what seems to me to be the greatest cause in the world today . . . That cause is to help the President keep the United States out of war."[288]

On December 17, Roosevelt revealed at a press conference his plans to provide billions of dollars in war supplies to Great Britain in the form of Lend-Lease (eventually, the U.S. would supply England with $13 billion). Joe expressed privately his feeling of having been exploited by the President. He started to sift his diplomatic papers in order to write a memoir of his London years, and told his friend and former president Herbert Hoover that the book would "put an entirely different color on the process of how America got into the war and would prove the betrayal of the American people by Franklin D. Roosevelt." But, Beschloss comments, "the necessities of wartime unity and, later, his sons' political careers kept Joseph Kennedy's diplomatic memoir out of print, where it remained."[289]

Kennedy left politics and devoted his remaining influence to his sons' political future. He stayed in relatively good terms with Roosevelt, although he refused to support his nomination for a fourth term, when he visited him, a very sick man, on October 26, 1944 in the White House. Kennedy recorded in his notes telling the President that the Catholic voters were hesitant to vote for him because "they felt that Roosevelt was Jew controlled." He added that he agreed "with the group who felt that the Hopkins, Rosenmans, and Frankfurters, and the rest of the incompetents would rob Roosevelt of the place in history that he hoped, I am sure, to have. . . . Roosevelt went on to say 'Why, I don't see Frankfurter twice a year.' And I said to him, 'You see him twenty times a day but you don't know it because he works through all these other groups of people without your knowing it.'"[290]

John Kennedy's intellectual filiation

John has always been loyal to his father's memory, and there is enough evidence that he shared his most fundamental principles. In 1940, John had published a book titled *Why England Slept,* adapted from his Harvard thesis which was, as the title alluded, a response to Churchill's 1938 book *While England Slept,* and a veiled support for his father's pro-appeasement views. Like his father, Kennedy never saw Hitler as an evil man, let alone as the man responsible for World War II. In 1942, aged 24, he was deeply in love with Inga Arvad, a Danish woman of stunning beauty and intelligence, who was a big fan of Hitler — her apartment had been bugged by FBI director Hoover on the suspicion that she was a Nazi spy.[291] Her biographer believes that no other woman had had more intellectual influence on JFK.[292] In 1945, John had predicted in his diary that, "within a few years Hitler will emerge from the hatred that surrounds him now as one of the most significant figures who ever lived. . . . he had a mystery about him in the way he lived and in the manner of his death that will live and grow after him. He had in him the stuff of which legends are made."[293] In 1956, in his book *Profiles in Courage,* John praised Senator Robert Taft for having, at tremendous personal cost, denounced in 1946 the hanging of eleven Nazi officials as motivated by "the spirit of vengeance" and as "a blot on the American record which we shall long regret."[294]

As James Douglass shows in *JFK and the Unspeakable,* President Kennedy was a peacemaker. He believed that "the primary function of the president of the United States [was] to keep the country out of war."[295] His horror of war was deep-seated. Although himself a genuine war hero with a well-deserved Navy and Marine Medal for "extremely heroic conduct," he wrote regretfully in his journal: "War will exist until that distant day when the conscientious objector enjoys the same reputation and prestige that the warrior does today."[296]

In 1945, JFK was a young journalist covering the founding conference of the United Nations in San Francisco. His biographer Chris Matthews writes:

> When Victory in Europe Day came — on May 8, during the conference's second week — Jack responded by writing eloquently in the *Herald-American:* "Any man who had risked his life for his country and seen his friends killed around him must inevitably wonder why this has happened to him and most important what good will it do. . . . it is not surprising that they should question the worth of their sacrifice and feel somewhat betrayed." / In a letter to one of his war buddies, he phrased his message more bluntly: "We must face the truth that the people have not been horrified by war to a sufficient extent to force them to go to any extent rather than have another war." . . . "The war makes less sense to me now," Jack wrote [in his journal], "than it

ever made and that was little enough — and I would really like —
as my life's goal . . . to do something to help prevent another."[297]

When announcing his candidacy for Congress on April 22,
1946, Kennedy declared: "Above all, day and night, with every
ounce of ingenuity and industry we possess, we must work for
peace. We must not have another war."[298] Hugh Sidey, one of his
journalist friends, wrote about him: "If I had to single out one
element in Kennedy's life that more than anything else influenced
his later leadership it would be a horror of war, a total revulsion
over the terrible toll that modern war had taken on individuals,
nations, and societies, and the even worse prospects in the nuclear
age. . . . It ran even deeper than his considerable public rhetoric on
the issue."[299] The exact same thing could have been said about his
father, who had been repulsed by the industrial butcheries of the
First World War. Joe had wanted to be — and had been in the eyes
of many — a peace hero. He had wanted peace as passionately as
Churchill had wanted war — total war.

Perhaps one of the clearest indications of John Kennedy's
profound intellectual filiation with his father is his invitation of
Charles Lindbergh on May 11, 1962, for a grand reception at the
White House. Lindbergh and his wife dined at the presidential
table and stayed overnight at the White House.[300] Their appearance
caused a sensation. Let's recall that, in September 1940, Lindbergh
had been a founding member of the America First Committee and
the staunchest critic of Roosevelt's ploys to drag the U.S. into the
war.[301] His reputation had suffered tremendously from his criticism
of Jewish influence, and he had been living as a recluse ever since.

Kennedy had nothing to gain politically from inviting him very
publicly to the White House. The significance of this gesture
should not be underestimated. It probably demonstrates a wish to
vindicate the vilified appeasers of 1938-40. Lindbergh at the White
House may have been a sign that the wheel was turning, and that
history would soon be written in a more balanced, appeased way.
John's assassination halted and reversed this movement. Half a
decade later, along with the expansion of Israel, the dark cult of the
Holocaust would start spreading across the U.S. and the world.
Arguably, if Kennedy had lived, there would be no compulsory
Holocaust religion today.

The Umbrella Man

In the first chapter of this book, we have seen how absurd and dishonest is the notion that Robert Kennedy was assassinated because he was "pro-Israel". In our second chapter, we have seen that his brother John Kennedy had become an object of deep resentment by the Israeli leadership. "In Ben-Gurion's eyes, John F. Kennedy was clearly a modern-day Haman — an enemy of the Jewish people," wrote Michael Collins Piper.[302] In the present chapter, if we have proven anything, it is that no collective entity hated the Kennedys more than Zionist Jews. For those whose self-image and worldview revolve around the Holocaust, the Kennedy brothers are essentially sons of a Hitler-appeaser and Nazi-supporter, and their leadership of the United-States is an existential threat as well as an intolerable insult. Although, for obvious reasons, this murderous hatred is seldom expressed publicly (John Podhoretz's "A Conversation in Hell" being a remarkable exception), it is a critical fact to take into account in our quest to solve the mystery of the "Kennedy curse." And it sheds a bright light on one of the most bizarre aspects of JFK's assassination.

In his 1967 book titled *Six Seconds in Dallas: a micro-study of the Kennedy assassination proving that three gunmen murdered the President*, Josiah Thompson first drew attention to a character who can be seen on the Zapruder film and on other photographs taken in Dealey Plaza at the moment of JFK's assassination. Here is how Thompson presents him in a short video recorded by Errol Morris for the *New York Times* in 2011:

> On November 22nd, it rained the night before. But everything cleared by about 9 or 9:30 in the morning. So if you were looking at various photographs of the motorcade route, in the crowd gathered there, you will have noticed: nobody is wearing a raincoat, nobody has an open umbrella. Why? Because it's a beautiful day. And then I noticed: in all of Dallas, there appears to be exactly one person standing under and open black umbrella. And that person is standing where the shots began to rain into the limousine. Let us call him "the umbrella man". . . . You can see him in certain frames from the Zapruder film, standing right there by the Stemmons Freeway sign. There are other still photographs taken from other locations in Dealey Plaza, which show the whole man standing under an open black umbrella — the only person under any umbrella in all of Dallas, standing right at the location where all the shots come into the limousine. Can any one come up with a non-sinister explanation for this? So I published this in *Six*

Seconds, but didn't speculate about what it meant … Well, I asked that the umbrella man come forward and explain this. So he did. He came forward and he went to Washington with his umbrella, and he testified in 1978 before the House Select Committee on Assassinations. He explained then why he had opened the umbrella and was standing there that day. The open umbrella was a kind of protest, a visual protest. It wasn't a protest of any of John Kennedy's policies as president. It was a protest at the appeasement policy of Joseph P. Kennedy, John Kennedy's father when he was ambassador to the court of Saint James in 1938 and 39. It was a reference to Neville Chamberlain's umbrella.[303]

The umbrella man was Louie Steven Witt, and had been identified by neighbors and local newsmen before he came forward to the HSCA. His explanation makes sense: the black umbrella was so much the iconic trademark of Prime Minister Neville Chamberlain that cartoonist David Low of the *London Evening Standard*, not only systematically drew him with his umbrella, but even drew him once *as* an umbrella! Since Chamberlain's return from Munich, his umbrella had become the symbol of appeasement, both for those who supported it (some old ladies "suggested that Chamberlain's umbrella be broken up and pieces sold as sacred relics")[304] and for those who opposed it ("Wherever Chamberlain traveled, the opposition party in Britain protested his appeasement at Munich by displaying umbrellas," according to Edward Miller).[305]

Josiah Thompson assumes that the Umbrella Man's bizarre behavior and JFK's assassination are unrelated, and that they happened at the exact same time and place by some kind of quantum-physics coincidence. He cannot bring himself to see the connection, even though the Umbrella Man himself made it clear to the HSCA that he wanted to heckle JFK about his father's appeasement of Hitler in 1938. Knowing what we know about Jewish perception of the "Kennedy curse" as linked to the "sins of the father", we cannot but find Thompson's refusal to see anything conspiratorial as very typical of Gentile self-induced blindness.

Was Louie Steven Witt a Zionist agent, a *sayan*? Not necessarily. He might have been instructed to do what he did without knowing that Kennedy would be killed right in front of him. Perhaps he did it for money, or perhaps as a service to his Jewish boss at the Rio Grande National Life insurance Co where he worked.

On the other hand, the explanation he gave for his "bad joke" sounds disingenuous: "In a coffee break conversation someone had mentioned that the umbrella was a sore spot with the Kennedy family. . . . I was just going to kind of do a little heckling." Witt carefully avoided mentioning why the umbrella was "a sore spot with the Kennedy family." He also avoided naming Joe Kennedy when he said that he had heard that "some members of the Kennedy family" had once been offended in an airport by people brandishing umbrellas. The "airport" sounds like an allusive reference to Chamberlain's widely publicized return at the Heston Aerodrome on 30 September 1938. There is clearly a cryptic undertone in Witt's explanation, which indicates a wish to convey a message for those who have ears to hear, but with enough vagueness for a plausible denial.

John Kennedy being heckled with Chamberlain's umbrella at the very moment he was being assassinated strikes me as a typical signature of the Zionist-Irgun mafia. The Umbrella Man is comparable to the line written by one of the murderers of the Tsar family on a wall in the house where they were murdered in 1918. The line was taken from a poem by Jewish author Heinrich Heine, relating how, in the Book of Daniel, the king of Babylon Belshazzar (intentionally misspelt *Belsatzar* by the Bolshevik assassin) saw "the writing on the wall" foretelling his destruction, and was killed as punishment for his offences against Israel's God.

Today, the Romanovs are canonized as "Holy Imperial Martyrs," with their own church built on the site of their slaughter. If we think of what the cult of the Romanovs means for Russia today, how it accompanies the rebirth of Russian civilization, we may start to understand how important the truth about the Kennedys is for America.

CHAPTER 7
JFK Jr., the Slain Prince

On July 16, 1999, John Fitzgerald Kennedy Junior was flying his private Piper Saratoga II, with his wife Carolyn Bessette and his sister-in-law Lauren Bessette. He was to drop Lauren off at Martha's Vineyard, then fly on with Carolyn to Hyannis Port for the wedding of his cousin Rory Kennedy the following day. At 9:39, as he was approaching Martha's Vineyard airport, John radioed the control tower for landing instructions, giving no sign of difficulty. At 9:41 p.m., John's plane suddenly plummeted into the ocean at the radar-recorded speed of 4,700 feet per minute. The next day, pieces of luggage from the plane were found floating nearly two miles away from the point of last radar contact.

On June 7, 2000, eleven months after the plane crash, the National Transportation Safety Board (NTSB) released its final report. That report was announced to the press by a short official NTSB news release which included the following statement: "The probable cause of the accident, as stated in the accident report, is: 'The pilot's failure to maintain control of the airplane during a descent over water at night, which was a result of spatial disorientation. Factors in the accident were haze and the dark night.'"[306]

The mainstream media distorted that brief statement to make its hesitant conclusion ("probable cause") more assertive and dramatic. "Haze and the dark night," mentioned as "factors in the accident," were exaggerated and declared totally unsafe for flying. "The pilot's failure to maintain control . . . as a result of spatial disorientation," became proof that JFK Jr. was incompetent to fly in such terrible weather at night. And the implication was that JFK Jr. was reckless and irresponsible to fly that night, especially with his wife and sister-in-law on board. But the main point of this narrative was to dismiss any suspicion of foul play by saying: given the weather and the pilot's experience, the accident was bound to happen.

Both these assertions — on weather conditions and visibility, and on the pilot's experience and cautiousness — are based on dubious testimonies. One key witness brought forward by the corporate media to support their claim of fatal visibility was Kyle Bailey, "the last man to see Kennedy alive at the Fairfield airport." He claims to have seen John take off that day and then "feared the combination of darkness and haze could be treacherous, causing him to lose sight of the horizon, lose his bearings, maybe even lose control of his plane."[307] It happens that Kyle Bailey soon became an aviation analyst regularly working for major network and cable televisions such as Fox News, CBS, ABC, NBC, BBC.[308] Bailey even appeared in the documentary *Curse on the Kennedys?* and more recently in the ABC documentary *The Last Days of JFK Jr.*, aired in January 2019, in which he repeats his uncorroborated story.

In *The Last Days of JFK Jr.* appears another character that fits what may be called the "Mark Walsh type"[309]: a private pilot by the name of Bob Arnot, who claims to have flown the same night along the same route as John. He too insists on the fatal fog, which made the lights of Martha's Vineyard invisible from the sky. You can read on Wikipedia that Arnot "is a journalist, author, former host of the *Dr. Danger* reality TV series, and previously medical and foreign correspondent for NBC and CBS." What a coincidence that those two key witnesses are TV professionals!

But Martha's Vineyard tower manager Marvin Wyatt is quoted in the NTSB report as saying visibility was great (contradicting the report's general conclusion). As for John Jr.'s lack of experience and recklessness, they are contradicted by all his friends, as well as by the NTSB report itself, which states that he had a flight experience of "about 310 hours, of which 55 hours were at night." During the last fifteen months, he had made 35 flights between Fairfield airport, N.J., and Martha's Vineyard, including five at night. Three certified flight instructors (CFI) quoted in the report describe John as an "excellent", "methodical" and "very cautious" pilot. In the early days, some newspapers echoed that view with their own research. John McColgan, JFK Jr.'s federal licensing instructor from Vero Beach, Florida, was interviewed for the *Orlando Sentinel*, July 18, 1999, and said: "He was an excellent pilot. . . . In fact, by now he probably has enough hours to be a commercial pilot."[310]

Jeb Burnside, commercial pilot and editor-in-chief of *Aviation Safety Magazine*, did a careful analysis of the NTSB report and radar data and confirms that weather conditions and pilot experience (or lack of) fail to explain the crash: "On paper, this accident shouldn't have happened. Despite most of his time being in a training environment, a typical 310-hour instrument-rating student in a well-equipped airplane should have had no problem with this flight."[311] This is in stark contradiction to the motif of "fatality" that later became the standard narrative.

But media distortion is not the most troublesome aspect of the case. The NTSB report itself conspicuously ignores the hypothesis of foul play. Many facts and testimonies inconsistent with the official explanation have been concealed, while some convenient ones seem to have been fabricated. Independent investigators have found enough omissions and contradictions in the official narrative to ask: Was JFK Jr., in fact, assassinated?

I am not going to review all the evidence of a cover-up. I refer you to my longer unz.com article, which is based on several web articles (including by early researchers such as John Quinn), chapter 7 of Donald Jeffries's good book *Hidden History: An Expose of Modern Crimes, Conspiracies, and Cover-Ups in American Politics* (2016),[312] and John Koerner, *Exploding the Truth: The JFK Jr., Assassination* (2018), which adds little. In addition, John Hankey's video "Dark Legacy II: the Assassination of JFK Jr" is very useful. However, I consider Koerner's Part I and Hankey's first 15 minutes, meant to blame the Bushs, as misleading.

Here are a few facts. The sudden nose-dive of JFK Jr.'s plane cannot be explained simply by an engine failure, as the *Boston Globe* correctly asserted four days after the crash: "Even if the engine died, a federal aviation source said, it is unlikely that the plane would reach such a high rate of descent, because the plane is designed to glide without power at a much slower rate for several miles. And if Kennedy had run out of fuel, it is likely he would have made a distress call."[313] The most likely explanation, apart from suicide, is that the plane suffered a structural damage, possibly by explosive, making it impossible to maintain in the air; blowing off a part of a wing or the tail would have been enough, and would have required only a very small device fixed to the plane.

Until June 19, there were many reports about John's perfectly normal call at 9:39, including a phone interview by Coast Guard Petty Officer Todd Burgun.[314] It was only the next day that FAA and NTSB officials produced some "newly found" radar "evidence" which supposedly showed Kennedy's flight exhibiting signs of difficulties and irregularities long before 9:39. Since Kennedy's perfectly normal call at 9:39 did not fit with that new version of events, it was never mentioned again, and Todd Burgun became unreachable.

The second element to consider is the testimony of Victor Pribanic, a trial lawyer from White Oak, Pennsylvania, who was fishing for striped bass off Squibnocket Point that night. He gave an interview to *The Martha's Vineyard Times,* cited in the *New York Daily News,* July 21, 1999: "I heard an explosion over my right shoulder. It sounded like an explosion. There was no shock wave, but it was a large bang." He also said, according to the *Daily News,* "that just before hearing the noise, he noticed a small aircraft flying low over the water toward the island."[315]

Finally, suspicions of foul play are reinforced by the fact that the search and recovery operations were conducted by the Air

Force and the Navy under national security conditions. No civilians or journalists were allowed in this area until the bodies and wreckage were recovered, and no one was able to see them afterwards. News reports were strictly controlled from the Pentagon. Autopsies were rushed, and the bodies were cremated in Duxbury's cemetery crematorium. Then their remains were taken aboard the Navy destroyer Briscoe, and scattered into the sea, near the place where they had found their death. This is hard to comprehend, since none of the plane passengers had ever served in the Navy, and cremation was not in the tradition of either family. It seems unconceivable that JFK Jr. would not have wished to be buried near his father.

According to information found in RFK Jr.'s diary, published by the *New York Post,* Ann Freeman, Carolyn and Lauren Bessette's mother, "began asking that her two daughters be buried near her home in Greenwich, Connecticut," but Edwin Schlossberg, Caroline Kennedy's Jewish husband, "bullied, bullied, bullied the shattered grieving mother," to convince her to have her two daughters cremated and their ashes spread in the ocean.[316] What was Schlossberg's motive? More importantly, what may have been the motive for John's murder?

JFK Jr. and the Camelot legacy

John Junior was literally born with the Kennedy presidency, precisely 17 days after his dad won the election. From the minute he came into this world, he had been in the national spotlight. As Americans watched him grow up in the White House, they developed a strong affection for him, which did not displease his father.

Little John turned three the day of his father's funeral, and he broke the world's heart when he solemnly saluted the President's coffin. That iconic image encapsulated a nation's grief, and impressed on millions of Americans the dream of seeing him reclaim the Oval Office one day. For in the American collective psyche, the Kennedys represented royalty, and JFK Jr. was the legitimate heir to the throne.

He was, wrote *the New York Daily News* the day after his death, the "charismatic crown prince of America's royal family."[317] "He was the closest thing we had to a crown prince," says Chris Cuomo in the tribute film *I am JFK Jr.* (2016).

After their father's death, John and Caroline's uncle Bobby played the role of surrogate father for them. When Bobby was assassinated in his turn in June 1968, Jackie said: "If they are killing Kennedys, my kids are the number one targets. I want to get out of this country."[318] She married shipping magnate Aristotle Onassis, whose assets included a seventy-five-member, machine-gun-equipped security force.

Jackie wanted her son to grow up knowing who his father was. As early as 1967, writes biographer Christopher Andersen in *The Good Son,*

> Jackie made sure that John was constantly exposed to the people who knew John [President Kennedy] best — from longtime pals like Red Fay, Chuck Spalding, Oleg Cassini, Bill Walton, and his ubiquitous sidekick Dave Powers to such New Frontier stalwarts as Pierre Salinger, Theodore Sorensen, and Arthur Schlesinger Jr. These were the folks "who knew Jack well and the things Jack liked to do." As long as they were around, she reasoned, "each day John will be getting to know his father."[319]

In 1972, Jackie asked Pierre Salinger to join her and her children for a month: "I want you to spend an hour or an hour and a half a day with John Jr. and Caroline and explain everything about what their father did." And so Salinger did.[320] And so, although John hardly kept real remembrance of his father, he was constantly steeped in the memory of him: "Whenever another child was visiting," writes Andersen, "he would inevitably ask, 'Would you like to hear my father?' Then he turned to a small stack of records and selected one to play."[321]

John's craving for information about his father was never quenched. His French friend and biographer Olivier Royant reports that, when running his magazine *George,* John hired Jacques Lowe, JFK's official photographer, and kept questioning him about his father for hours.[322]

Even John's irresistible yearning for flying, despite his mother's plea not to do so, can possibly be traced back to his childhood, "when he and his mother watched as Daddy's helicopter took off from the South Lawn in 1962," or watched him reappear from the sky. When Nanny Shaw announced to little John in the morning of November 23, 1963, "John, your father has gone to heaven to take care of Patrick [JFK and Jackie's third child, who did not survive his first month]," John asked, "Did Daddy take his big plane with him?" "Yes," she answered. "I wonder," John said, "when he's coming back."[323] Significantly, John gave his first private plane the registration number N529JK, a reference to his father's May 29 birthday.

Jackie, the guiding spirit in John's life, definitely saw her son as Camelot's standard-bearer. In her last letter to him before dying to lymphoma in 1994, she wrote: "You, especially, have a place in history." [324] According to presidential historian Doug Wead, speaking in *I am JFK Jr.,* Jackie "knew in her heart that, some day, the stars are gonna line up, and he's gonna be president." "My mom sort of pressured me to get into politics," John told Lloyd Howard in 1997. "She expected me to follow in my father's footsteps, and of course I will. But I don't think the time is right just yet."[325]

In 1995, John launched his magazine *George.* Under the appearance of superficiality, it engaged in controversial issues of deep politics that reflected John's interests. His longtime friend Robert Littell wrote, in *The Men We Became: My Friendship with John F. Kennedy Jr.* (St. Martin's Press, 2004): "*George* was also an opportunity for John to build a platform from which he might possibly move into political life." After all, his father had also pursued a career in journalism before entering politics. *George* was also a means for John to interact with political actors and thinkers.

John didn't shun from letting people know his interest for his father's legacy. In October 1997, for the 35th anniversary of the Cuban Missile Crisis, John travelled to Cuba to meet Fidel Castro. The interview he had wished didn't materialize, but Castro invited him for dinner and for a swim in the Bay of Pigs, and rumor has it that Castro gave him his view on his father's death.[326] John's interest for the presidency transpired heavily in *George,* particularly in the section "If I were president," in which various personalities were asked for suggestions.

John's plans in 1999

In 1999, at age 39, John was trying to sell his magazine. He had new plans. According to Gary Ginsberg, a collaborator who was with John the night before he died, "That last night he was very focused on two things: finding a buyer for *George* and his political future."[327] Andersen writes in *The Good Son*: "There seemed little doubt in the minds of those who knew him that John was on the brink of a bright political future. 'He was probably a more natural politician than any of the other Kennedys,' David Halberstam said, 'and that includes his father. John had all the makings of a political superstar — once he decided that's what he wanted.'"

In July 1999, his decision was made. His closest friends have testified that he was preparing to enter an election contest. Pierre Salinger, who knew him well, declared on French radio Europe 1, on July 19, 1999: "I felt that in the coming year John Junior would also enter politics. . . . we thought he was going to be a Democratic candidate for the next presidential election."[328] More plausibly, John Jr. would first have sought a political office in New York State, where he had lived since 1963. He loved New York, and New York loved him. A 1997 private poll ranked JFK Jr. as New York's "most popular Democrat," giving him 65 percent approval rating among fellow Democrats.[329] John had several options. One he excluded was mayor of New York City. His assistant at *George*, RoseMarie Terenzio, recounts that when New York Senator Al D'Amato suggested he should run for mayor, John laughed it off, and later commented to Terenzio, "Well, Rosie, how many mayors do you know that became President?"[330] Terenzio's opinion is that John "would've run in 2008," while others, she said, thought "he would've waited for 2016. He would be 56."[331] In the meantime, according to Gary Ginsberg,

> He had been thinking about running for the N.Y. Senate seat — he even had meetings about it that spring — but by July had concluded he would focus his attention on running for governor of N.Y. in 2003. By temperament and interest, John, I think, realized he was far more suited to being a governor than a legislator. He knew from running *George* that he could be an inspiring, strong chief executive of a state, setting the tone for government and successfully running a complex operation. That idea became very appealing to him at some point that summer. Had the stars aligned over the next couple of years, I'm pretty convinced that's what he would have pursued."[332]

Steven Gillon, friend of John from their time at Brown University, expresses the same opinion in his recent book *The Life of John F. Kennedy Jr., America's Reluctant Prince* (2019): "he didn't want to be a legislator — he always saw himself as an executive. Maybe he would run for governor of New York."[333]

Others around John believed he was about to enter the race for the Senate seat that Daniel Moynihan, a former assistant to President Kennedy, was going leave vacant in 2000. This is the seat that Bobby Kennedy had occupied from 1964 to 1968. On July 19, 1999, *New York Daily News* reporter Joel Siegel interviewed two unnamed friends of JFK Jr., and wrote: "Earlier this year, in one of the best-kept secrets in state politics, Kennedy considered seeking the seat of retiring Sen. Daniel Moynihan in 2000, friends confirmed yesterday." "This is a guy who everybody recognized who would have had any nomination for the asking," commented Democratic Chairman John Marino, also quoted in Siegel's article.[334]

Christopher Andersen supports the view that, after consulting with Democratic leaders, John had made up his mind for the Senate. It clashed with Hillary Clinton's plan. The Clintons, who were to leave the White House in January 2001, were purchasing a home in Chappaqua, N.Y., and Hillary was gearing up to run for the Senate as a stepping-stone to the presidency.

> In the end, John was still convinced his best shot was at running for Moynihan's Senate seat. Hillary Clinton had hesitated to enter the race largely because she feared John, who was being touted behind the scenes as her principal rival for the nomination, would be a formidable foe. John was both heir to the Kennedy magic and *People*'s "Sexiest Man Alive," as well as the consummate New Yorker, a resident of the city since the age of three. Although New York had no residency requirements, Hillary, who had never spent more than a few days at a time in New York, would almost certainly be branded a carpetbagger. . . . In early July, Hillary finally made her move and formally announced her candidacy. But she was still concerned about the possibility that John might decide to toss his hat into the ring. As it turned out, she was right. John was now more confident than ever that he could easily beat her at the polls. He believed Hillary was vulnerable not only because of the Monica Lewinsky affair, her husband's subsequent impeachment, and a slew of brewing scandals in the Clinton White House, but mainly because she simply had no connection to the state he loved.[335]

Andersen then quotes from the testimony of John's longtime friend Billy Noonan, who authored in 2006 *Forever Young: My Friendship with John F. Kennedy, Jr.* (Viking Press). Here is what

Noonan writes precisely, referring to the last phone conversation he had with John, whom he was supposed to meet on July 16:

> He had been making vague references on the phone about shutting things down, and starting things up. During the week before our anniversary dinner, he told me that he had something pressing to talk about, but with curious ears in the office, John was cautious. "We'll talk about it this weekend." . . . I asked him now what was up with that [1997] poll, to rib him about how the press was pushing for Hillary Clinton to replace Moynihan. "Wait until she gets here," John said. "She's gonna get her head handed to her." He was in.[336]

This is the only mention by Noonan of John's intention to run for the Senate. On one hand, it is not much. On the other, it should be taken seriously, coming from one of John's most intimate friends. Given the importance of the issue, there can be no doubt that Noonan weighed every word he wrote. One gets the impression that he wanted to say what he knew for the record, yet felt restrained from saying it too clearly.

Reflecting a widely held opinion, Andrew Collins writes that Hilary "knew she could never defeat the son of JFK in New England," and had reasons to worry: "JFK Jr. had entered the political scene. New York was electric with word of JFK Jr. reclaiming his father's legacy! A piece of Camelot was still alive in America, and donors began to line up."[337] Hillary stood no chance if John ever stepped across her way, and that was sure to happen sooner or later. It is true, as some authors object, that John never frontally attacked the Clintons in his magazine *George,* perhaps out of Democratic loyalty. But one of the very last issues of *George* that he oversaw himself (April 1999) was hostile to Hillary's bid on the Senate seat, posting on the front-page: "Why Hillary won't be senator." In April 1996, the cover had: "Why Women Will Dump Hillary." But with John out of the way, Hillary did win the seat and, disturbingly, the November 1999 issue of *George* contained an exclusive interview of her, together with — in tragic irony — an article on "How Bobby Kennedy Seduced New York."

Based on all the testimonies quoted above, no certainty can be reached about John's immediate plan, other that he was at the dawn of a bright political future, that he had several options in New York State, and that his long term goal was the White House.

JFK Jr. as conspiracy theorist

According to testimonies from his friends, John Junior was haunted by the death of his father and quite knowledgeable about independent investigations contradicting the Warren Report. In 1999, he was not a newcomer to JFK conspiracy theories; his quest for truth had started as early as the late 1970s. His high school girlfriend Meg Azzoni writes in *11 Letters and a Poem* (2007) that as a teenager, JFK Jr. was questioning the official version of his father's death: "His heartfelt quest was to expose and bring to trial who killed his father, and covered it up."[338] Don Jeffries, author of *Hidden History,* claimed that "another friend of JFK, Jr.'s adult inner circle, who very adamantly requested to remain anonymous, verified that he was indeed quite knowledgeable about the assassination and often spoke of it in private."[339] JFK Jr., said Jeffries in a radio interview on midnightwriternews.com, was on "a Shakespearian quest," "to avenge his father's death," like young Hamlet.[340]

John is the only Kennedy to have shown a serious determination to pursue this truth, besides his uncle Bobby and, more recently, Bobby's elder son. And he took the risk of making his interest public in October 1998, when he released a special "Conspiracy Issue" of *George* magazine, which included an article by Oliver Stone titled "Our Counterfeit History," introduced on the cover as "Paranoid and Proud of It!" It must be recalled that Stone's film, despite its box-office success, had so far received only contempt from the media.

As many truth seekers who had started with the Kennedy assassination, John had developed an awareness that other events of great historical consequence were the subject of State-orchestrated lies and cover-ups, with corporate media complicity. And so the JFK assassination was not the only "conspiracy issue" explored by *George*. It is worth taking a look at two others, for they may inform us on the direction John Jr. was taking in his quest for truth.

In December 1996, *George* delved into the theory that TWA Flight 800, which had exploded on July 17, 1996 soon after leaving JFK International, had been downed by a missile, rather than as the result of an short-circuit near the central fuel tank, as the National Transportation Safety Board concluded. The claim was based on the testimonies of 375 witnesses who saw one or two bright flare objects hit the plane, many of them believing it was a missile (watch on YouTube the 2001 documentary *Silenced: TWA 800 and the Subversion of Justice*). The article supported Pierre Salinger, who had been the most prominent journalist arguing that TWA 800 was shot down by a missile fired from a U.S. Navy ship. Salinger was severely attacked by his peers, and his notoriety suffered permanent damage. But in May 27, 1999, he reaffirmed his belief and asked to be vindicated in a *Georgetowner* column, based on new research confirming his views.[341]

In March 1997, three months after the issue featuring the "TWA Conspiracy Theories" cover article, *George* magazine published a 13-page article by the mother of Yigal Amir, the man convicted of assassinating Israeli Prime Minister Yitzhak Rabin. Rabin had offended the Israeli far-right by wanting to trade land for peace. Amir's mother revealed that her son had operated under the tutelage and training of a Shin Bet agent, Avishai Raviv, working for forces seeking to halt the peace process.[342]

Conclusion

We have established the following two things:

1) At age 39, John had made up his mind to launch his political career by seeking an electoral mandate in New York State, and he was about to announce it publicly. He had expressed to his friends his ambition to ultimately reach for the presidency. Given his personality and his popularity, he had high chances to make it in less than 20 years. He might realistically have become U.S. President in 2008 or 2016.

2) Brought up in the worship of his father, John had taken a keen interest in JFK conspiracy theories at least since his late teens. His knowledge deepened in his thirties, made him aware of state and media cover-ups in other affairs, and motivated him to

publish, eight months before his death, a cover article by Oliver Stone, director of the groundbreaking film *JFK*, titled "Our Counterfeit History".

Those two things must be connected. John's quest for the truth about President Kennedy's assassination cannot be separated from his political ambition to reclaim the White House, anymore than it could be in the case of his uncle Bobby. These are two sides of the same destiny. The heir and the avenger are one and the same person.

So, was JFK Jr. himself assassinated? The evidence may not be compelling, but what can be proven beyond a reasonable doubt is that federal authorities and corporate media engaged in a systematic cover-up of any facts that contradicted the theory of the accident due to the pilot's error. And that is enough to decide between accident and assassination. The transgenerational cabal who had the motive, means and opportunity to murder JFK and RFK (and the power to get away with it) had the same motive, means and opportunity to murder JFK Jr. (and the same power to get away with it).

Here is a man whose road to the presidency seemed traced. No other man of his age had better chances to reach the White House one day. And no other man in the world had more reasons to want the 1963 Kennedy assassination reinvestigated. He was already trying to educate the public through his magazine, at the risk of exposing his own beliefs, something no other Kennedy had done before. And this man, his best friend Noonan believes, was just about to announce his candidacy for a New York Senate seat, which everyone would have understood as the first step toward the White House. What are the odds that he would die at this precise moment by accident? How lucky for his enemies! If that was an accident, then that alone deserves to be called a "Kennedy curse," doesn't it! If it was an accident, then the Devil caused it. Or was it Yahweh?

We have seen how close Jack and Bobby had been. A bond of spirit of a comparable nature existed between John F. Kennedy and the son that bore his name. Although John Junior could not speak with his father, nor even remember speaking with him, his love and loyalty to his father, nurtured by his mother, was the driving force in his life. From the point of view of JFK and RFK's murderers, JFK Jr. was a recurring nightmare, the returning ghost of both JFK and RFK. All three were like one man who had to be killed three times. JFK Jr. embodied the survival or the resurrection of a Kennedy legacy that refused to die. The Zionists saw that legacy as something to eradicate from U.S. political life altogether.

And if JFK Jr. had to be stopped, it make sense to kill him before he made his political ambitions public. After, the motive would be harder to conceal: most Americans might find a second heir to JFK killed on the road to the White House hard to swallow. Not to mention the problem that JFK Jr. may pose to the conspirators of 9/11: in view of his interest and knowledge in "conspiracy theories," one may wonder how he would have dealt with 9/11. Would *George* have been the only mainstream magazine to question the official narrative?

Besides, to let JFK Jr. live longer would be taking the risk of having a JFK III coming into this world: more trouble in perspective. Indeed, Carolyn may have been pregnant when she died with her husband.

But wait: there is still one male heir to John F. Kennedy: Jack Schlossberg, son of Caroline Kennedy and Edwin Schlossberg. Will he become "our first Jewish president," asks Rabbi Jeffrey Salkin?[343]

CHAPTER 8
Forrestal, Kennedy's Foreshadow

Israel as serial killer

Eliminating non-submissive foreign leaders is part of Israel's struggle for existence. Besides, it is entirely biblical: foreign kings are supposed to "lick the dust at [Israelis'] feet" (Isaiah 49:23), or perish, their names "blotted out under heaven" (Deuteronomy 7:24).

On November 6, 1944, members of the Stern Gang, led by future Prime Minister Yitzhak Shamir, assassinated Lord Moyne, the British resident minister in the Middle East, for his anti-Zionist positions. The bodies of his murderers, executed in Egypt, were later exchanged for twenty Arab prisoners and buried at the "Monument of Heroes" in Jerusalem.

On September 17, 1948, the same terrorist group murdered in Jerusalem Count Folke Bernadotte, a Swedish diplomat appointed as United Nations mediator in Palestine. He had just submitted his report A/648, which described "large-scale Zionist plundering and destruction of villages," and called for the "return of the Arab refugees rooted in this land for centuries." His assassin, Nathan

Friedman-Yellin, was arrested, convicted, and then amnestied; in 1960 he was elected to the Knesset.[344]

In 1946, members of the Irgun, led by future Prime Minister Menachem Begin, killed ninety-one people in the headquarter of the British Mandate's administration (King David Hotel). Three months later, the same terrorist group attempted to murder British Prime Minister Clement Attlee and Foreign Secretary Ernest Bevin, according to British Intelligence documents declassified in 2006.

These killings and more are documented by Israeli journalist Ronen Bergman in *Rise and Kill First: The Secret History of Israel's Targeted Assassination* (2018). Bergman writes: "At the end of 1947, a report to the British high commissioner tallied the casualties of the previous two years: 176 British Mandate personnel and civilians killed. 'Only these actions, these executions, caused the British to leave,' David Shomron said, decades after he shot Tom Wilkin dead on a Jerusalem street. 'If [Avraham] Stern had not begun the war, the State of Israel would not have come into being.'"[345]

Absent from Israel's body count in Bergman's book is former U.S. Secretary of Defense James Forrestal, assassinated eight months after Count Bernadotte. Forrestal had been Roosevelt's Secretary of the Navy from April 1944. With the consolidation of the armed services under Truman in 1947, he became the first Secretary of Defense. He opposed the United Nations' vote to partition Palestine, and protested vigorously against U.S. recognition of Israel on May 15, 1948, on the ground that U.S. interests in the Middle East would be seriously jeopardized by American sponsorship of a Jewish state. For this, Forrestal received "an outpouring of slander and calumny that must surely be judged one of the most shameful intervals in American journalism," in the words of Robert Lovett, then Under Secretary of State. Truman replaced Forrestal on March 28, 1949 — shortly after his reelection — by his main fundraiser, Louis Johnson. According to the received story, Forrestal, who was psychologically exhausted, fell into depression immediately. On April 2, 1949, he was interned against his will in the military hospital of the Navy in Bethesda, Maryland, where he was forcibly confined for seven weeks. He fell to his death from the 16th floor at 1:50 in the morning of May 22, 1949, landing on the roof of the third floor. He had a dressing-gown sash tied around his neck.

National authorities immediately labeled his death a suicide, without any criminal investigation. A review board was appointed on May 23, headed by Admiral Morton Willcutts, to conduct hearings of members of the hospital staff, with the purpose of exonerating everyone of responsibility in Forrestal's assumed suicide. The board completed its work in one week, and released a short press release four months later. The *New York Times* wrote, October 12, 1949: "Francis P. Matthews, Secretary of the Navy, made public today the report of an investigating board absolving all individuals of blame in the death of James Forrestal last May 22." But the full report, containing the transcripts of all hearings an crucial exhibits, was kept secret for 55 years, until David Martin obtained it through a Freedom of Information Act request in April 2004.[346]

In his book *The Assassination of James Forrestal* and in his web articles complementing it, David Martin makes a compelling case that Forrestal was murdered, and that his murder was ordered by the Zionists, possibly with the approval of Truman. I will here summarize the evidence, and highlight the significance of this case for our understanding of Israel's takeover of the heart, soul, and body of the United States. Unless specified otherwise, all information is from Martin's book or articles.[347]

My interest for this heartbreaking story stems from my interest for the Kennedy assassinations. I found the connection and similarities between the two stories illuminating. Everyone knows that Kennedy was assassinated, yet most Americans are still unaware of the evidence incriminating Israel. In the case of Forrestal, it is the opposite: few people suspect a murder, but once the evidence for murder has been presented, it points directly to Israel as the culprit. For this reason, Forrestal's assassination by the Zionists becomes a precedent that makes JFK's assassination by the same collective entity more plausible. If Israel can kill a former U.S. Defense Secretary on American soil in 1949 and get away with it with government and media complicity, then why not a sitting President fifteen years later?

Forrestal was of Irish Catholic origin like Joseph Kennedy, his contemporary and friend. Both men are examples of American patriots of Irish stock and Catholic upbringing who were alarmed by Jewish influence over American foreign policy. The entry for 27 December 1945 in Forrestal's edited diary, says: "Played golf with Joe Kennedy. I asked him about his conversations with

Roosevelt and Neville Chamberlain from 1938 on. . . . Chamberlain, he says, stated that America and the world Jews had forced England into the war."

When James Forrestal, hostile to Stalin's ambitions on Eastern Europe and to Truman's decision to nuke Japan, was kept away from the official delegation to the Potsdam Conference in the summer 1945, he flew there privately and took with him the then 28-year-old John Kennedy, for a tour of post-war Germany. Later on, John integrated James's son Michael Forrestal as a member of his National Security Council. In May 1963 he visited the grave of James Forrestal on Memorial Day.

James Forrestal's and John Kennedy's assassinations bear one sinister thing in common: Bethesda Naval Hospital. As most readers recall, this is where Kennedy's fraudulent autopsy was produced after his body had been whisked away at gunpoint from Dallas Parkland Hospital, most probably by Secret Service agents on Lyndon Johnson's order. The report of this autopsy stated that the fatal bullet had entered the back of Kennedy's skull. This contradicted the observation of surgeon Charles Crenshaw, who is adamant that "the bullet had entered his head through the front," as also testified twenty-one doctors, nurses and Secret Service agents at Parkland Hospital — which exonerates Oswald, who was behind the President at the time of the shooting.[348]

In 1963, Johnson had his own men in the Navy: it was Johnson who obtained from Kennedy the nomination of Texan senator John Connally as Navy Secretary in 1961, then of Fred Korth, another of his Texan friends, in 1962. Johnson's control over the Navy may have something to do with Bethesda Navy Hospital performing the fraudulent autopsy.

It happens that Johnson makes a special appearance, although brief and poorly documented, in the story of Forrestal's assassination. LBJ was then a newly elected congressman on the payroll of Abraham Feinberg. According to Forrestal's assistant Marx Leva, Johnson paid an unwanted visit to Forrestal at Bethesda Hospital. David Martin asks: "Could LBJ have been playing something of a foot-soldier role for the orchestrators of Forrestal's demise? Might he have been there to size up the overall situation, and at the same time contribute to 'making his bones,' as it were, by participating in such an important operation?"[349]

Was Forrestal suicidal?

No criminal investigation was conducted into the death of James Forrestal, either by the FBI or the NCIS (Navy Criminal Investigative Service). The very day of his death, the press announced his suicide as a matter of fact. The *New York Times* stated in its late May 22 edition that Forrestal "jumped thirteen stories to his death," and added the next morning: "There were indications that Mr. Forrestal might also have tried to hang himself. The sash of his dressing-gown was still knotted and wrapped tightly around his neck when he was found, but hospital officials would not speculate as to its possible purpose."

Later biographers did speculate that he may have tried to hang himself but failed to tie the sash securely to the radiator beneath the window. In *The Man Who Kept the Secrets,* Pulitzer Price winner Thomas Powers says — with unconscious black humor — that Forrestal died trying to hang himself "from his hospital window, but slipped and fell sixteen stories to his death."

Forrestal left no suicide note, but the *New York Times* (May 23) informs its readers that: "A book of poetry beside his bed was opened to a passage from the Greek tragedian, Sophocles, telling of the comfort of death. . . . Mr. Forrestal had copied most of the Sophocles poem from the book on hospital memo paper, but he had apparently been interrupted in his efforts. His copying stopped after he had written 'night' of the word 'nightingale' in the twenty-sixth line of the poem."

On May 24, the *New York Times* gave the final word to the psychiatrist in charge, who made Forrestal's suicide sound predictable: "Captain George M. Raines, the Navy psychiatrist who had been treating Mr. Forrestal, said that the former Secretary ended his life in a sudden fit of despondency. He said this was 'extremely common' to the patient's severe type of mental illness."

That's it. Never did any reporter hint at the possibility of foul play. The conclusion that Forrestal's death is an obvious suicide caused by his "mental illness" was taken at face value by the authors of Forrestal's two main biographies: Arnold Rogow, *James Forrestal, A Study of Personality, Politics, and Policy* (MacMillan Company, 1963); and Townsend Hoopes and Douglass Brinkley, *Driven Patriot, the Life and Times of James Forrestal* (Alfred A. Knopf, 2003).

Rogow, whose book has been called a "psychological autopsy," insists on linking Forrestal's alleged mental illness to his alleged anti-Semitism. Rogow is an expert on the subject of anti-Semitism, on which he wrote the article for *The International Encyclopedia of Social Science*. He is also the author of *The Jew in a Gentile World: An Anthology of Writings about Jews by Non-Jews*.

Hoopes and Brinkley borrow heavily from Rogow, but add valuable information based on their own interviews. They give an interesting interpretation of the morbid poem allegedly copied by Forrestal from Mark Van Dorren's *Anthology of World Poetry*, titled "The Chorus from Ajax." Taking their clue from Zionist apologist John Loftus, author of *The Belarus Secret* (1982), they speculate that, when reaching the word "nightingale" in the poem, Forrestal might have been overwhelmed by a sudden rush of guilt for having authorized a CIA operation with the code name of "Nightingale," that infiltrated into the Soviet Union Ukrainian spies who were former Nazi collaborators and probably killers of Jews. The word "nightingale," Hoopes and Brinkley surmise, must have triggered Forrestal's urge to take the poet's admonition literally and end his life on the spot.

David Martin has uncovered grave inconsistencies and outright lies in the official story. First, it appears that Forrestal's nervous breakdown has been wildly exaggerated, if not totally invented. As the story goes, Forrestal's mental health had started deteriorating before Truman replaced him, and collapsed on March 29, just after a brief ceremony in his honor at Capitol Hill. The main source for this story is an oral history interview of Marx Leva, Forrestal's special assistant at that time, recorded for the Truman Library in 1969. In a strangely self-serving passage, Leva says that, on that day, he found Forrestal in his Pentagon office, "almost in a coma." He had him driven home and later met him there with Forrestal's friend Ferdinand Eberstadt, and the two men decided that Forrestal's state required that he urgently take some vacation. So Leva made immediate arrangement for a Marine plane to fly him to the estate of Robert Lovett in Hobe Sound, Florida that very night. "And on the way out Forrestal said three times . . . 'You're a loyal fellow, Marx.'" Since Leva is Jewish, the implication is that Forrestal was obsessed by the disloyalty he attributed to some Jewish officials. For Leva, "he apparently was beyond being neurotic, I mean it was apparently paranoid."[350]

David Martin shows in an additional article that Marx Leva is lying: Forrestal's vacation had in fact been planned in advance, and his wife was already waiting for him there.[351] This is proven by a *Jacksonville Daily Journal* article dated March 28, relating the ceremony when Truman pinned the Distinguished Service Medal on Forrestal's chest that very day. The article concludes: "Forrestal is flying tomorrow to Hobe Sound, Fla., for a long rest." A video clip of Forrestal shows him perfectly healthy and composed on March 28.[352]

News reports and biographies insist that, during his four-day stay at Hobe Sound, Forrestal showed signs of paranoia. One rumor, made up by Daniel Yergin and repeated by Thomas Powers in *The Man Who Kept the Secrets,* has him running through the streets yelling, "The Russians are coming." There is no credible source for this claim. Under Secretary of State (and future Defense Secretary) Robert Lovett, who was at Hobe Sound with Forrestal, did say in 1974 that Forrestal appeared to him as "not of sound mind," because "he was obsessed with the idea that his phone calls were being bugged," and complained that "they're really after me." I find rather strange, though, that Lovett feigns to ignore who Forrestal meant by "they". There is nothing irrational in Forrestal's belief that "his telephones were being bugged, [and that] his house was being watched", as he had earlier complained to Truman's appointments secretary, Matthew J. Connelly (who said so in a 1968 interview for the Truman Library).[353]

There is also a rumor that Forrestal attempted suicide at Hobe Sound. It is contradicted by the Willcutts report, in which Dr. George Raines, the psychiatrist in charge of Forrestal at Bethesda, is recorded stating: "So far as I know he never made a single real attempt at suicide except that one that was successful." All of Forrestal's doctors interviewed are unanimous that he had never attempted suicide before his fatal fall.

That is not to say that Forrestal was not psychologically strained in 1949. As Secretary of Defense, he had been subjected not only to slander and calumny by the press, but also to anonymous death threats. Robert Lovett, who shared Forrestal's views on Israel, testified that he himself received night phone calls with death threats, and that Forrestal was more exposed than him to this kind of treatment. Having lost all protection from the government after March 28, Forrestal had reasons to fear for his life. On May 23, 1949, *The Washington Post* concluded an article headlined "Delusions of Persecution, Acute Anxiety, Depression Marked Forrestal's Illness," with the somewhat paradoxical statement: "His fear of reprisals from pro-Zionists was said to stem from attacks by some columnists on what they said was his opposition to partition of Palestine under a UN mandate. In his last year as Defense Secretary, he received great numbers of abusive and threatening letters."

John Loftus and Mark Aarons, the arch-Zionist authors of *The Secret War against the Jews,* identify Forrestal as "the principal villain, the man who nearly succeeded in preventing Israel's birth." They reveal that "The Zionists had tried unsuccessfully to blackmail Forrestal with tape recordings of his own deals with the Nazis" (before the war, Forrestal had been a partner of Clarence Dillon, the Jewish founder of the banking firm Dillon, Read, and Co.), but they believe that Zionist harassment at least succeeded in making him insane: "His paranoia convinced him that his every word was bugged. To his many critics, it seemed that James Forrestal's anti-Jewish obsession had finally conquered him."[354] How convenient to claim that anti-Semitism may lead to suicide. When the Zionist mafia wishes you dead, is fearing for your life a sign of mental illness?

We need not doubt Raines's words to the Willcutts Review Board that, when he first saw Forrestal at Bethesda Hospital, "he was obviously exhausted physically" and showed "high blood pressure." But here, we also have to take into account that Forrestal had been literally abducted from his vacation center at Hobe Sound. We are not surprised when Rogow, and Hoopes and Brinkley after him, tell us that, even though he had been sedated, Forrestal "was in a state of extreme agitation during the flight from Florida," and that: "Forrestal's agitation increased during the trip in a private car from the airfield to the hospital. He made several attempts to leave the car while it was in motion, and had to be forcibly restrained. Arriving at Bethesda, he declared that he did not expect to leave the hospital alive." As Martin mentions, there is also the very real possibility that Forrestal had been drugged at Hobe Sound, in order to make him appear insane and justify his internment.

Forrestal's behavior at Bethesda shows nothing abnormal for a man locked up in the psychiatric division of a military hospital, for reasons he feared were not strictly medical. It has been reported by medical personnel that Forrestal often seemed restless, walking back and forth in his room late at night. Why wouldn't he? Forrestal was even denied visits by those dearest to him. His brother Henry had tried several times to visit him, but had been rebuffed by Dr. Raines. The hospital authorities relented only after Henry threatened legal action. Forrestal was also denied the visit of his friend the Catholic priest Maurice Sheehy. Sheehy wrote in *The Catholic Digest,* January 1951, that, "The day he was admitted to the hospital, Forrestal told Dr. Raines he wished to see me," but that Dr. Raines told him "that Jim was so confused I should wait some days before seeing him." Raines turned away Father Sheehy on six occasions.

Despite being kept in virtual imprisonment and under forced medication, Forrestal endured remarkably well. From the hearings conducted by the Willcutts Review Board, it appears that he was doing fine, in the days preceding his death. Willcutts himself expressed surprise at learning about his death, because he had dinner with him one day earlier (Friday 20), and thought he was "getting along splendidly."

Strangely enough, the Willcutts Review Board's report states that Forrestal's fall was the cause of his death, but avoids any statement about the cause of the fall itself. It shows an obvious lack of interest regarding all elements that point to murder rather than to suicide. The nurse who first entered Forrestal's room after his death testified that there was broken glass on his bed. But the room must have been laundered before the crime scene photographs were taken, because they show the bed with nothing but a bare mattress, while another picture shows broken glass on the carpet at the foot of his bed.[355] The Willcutts Board had no interest in finding the origin of the broken glass, nor the reason it was removed from the bed.

They also failed to raise any questions about the gown sash tied around Forrestal's neck. Hoopes and Brinkley later speculated that Forrestal tied the sash to a radiator beneath the window, but that his knot "gave way." That is contradicted by hospital corpsman William Eliades, who found the body of Forrestal with the sash around his neck, and declared to the Willcutts Review Board: "I looked to see whether he had tried to hang himself and whether a piece of cord had broken off. It was still in one piece except it was tied around his neck."

But the most compelling proof that Forrestal's death has been disguised as a suicide is the poem allegedly copied by Forrestal.

Among the exhibits obtained by Martin alongside the Willcutts report is a copy of the memo sheet with the transcription of the poem. A comparison with any handwritten note by Forrestal makes it plain that it was not copied by Forrestal.[356]

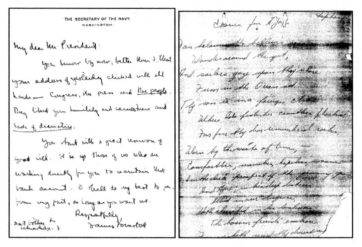

Interestingly, no one is identified in the official report as the discoverer of this handwritten note. It didn't occur to the members of the Review Board to mention how it came into their possession, and to question the person who gave it to them.

Was it the Communists or the Zionists?

Before David Martin, one author, writing under the penname Cornell Simpson, had claimed that Forrestal had been murdered. His book, *The Death of James Forrestal,* was published in 1966, although he claims to have written it in the mid-1950s. Simpson's book contains much valuable and credible information. He had for example interviewed James Forrestal's brother Henry, who was positively certain that his brother had been murdered. Henry Forrestal found the timing of the death very suspicious because he was coming to take his brother out of the hospital a few hours later that very same day. According to Simpson, another person who didn't believe in Forrestal's suicide was Father Maurice Sheehy. When he hurried to the hospital several hours after Forrestal's death, he was approached discreetly by an officer who whispered to him, "Father, you know Mr. Forrestal didn't kill himself, don't you?"

Simpson blames the Communists for Forrestal's murder. The claim is not preposterous. Forrestal was definitely anti-communist. He had been alarmed by what he saw as Communist infiltration in the Roosevelt administration (the Venona Decrypts, giving evidence of 329 Soviet agents inside the U.S. government during World War II, would prove him right). After Roosevelt's death, he was influential in the transformation of U.S. policy toward the Soviet Union, from accommodation to "containment". Senator Joseph McCarthy, another Irish Catholic, testifies in his book *The Fight for America* (1952) that it was Forrestal who directly inspired his exposés of Communist influence and subversion in the federal government: "Before meeting Jim Forrestal I thought we were losing to international Communism because of incompetence and stupidity on the part of our planners. I mentioned that to Forrestal. I shall forever remember his answer. He said, 'McCarthy, consistency has never been a mark of stupidity. If they were merely stupid they would occasionally make a mistake in our favor.' This phrase stuck me so forcefully that I have often used it since."

Strangely, McCarthy also died in Bethesda Hospital, at the age of 48 (May 2, 1957). The death certificate reads "hepatitis, acute, cause unknown," and the doctors declared that the inflammation of the liver was of a "noninfectious type". Acute hepatitis can be caused either by infection or by poisoning, yet no autopsy was performed. Simpson comments (as quoted at length in Martin's article "James Forrestal and Joe McCarthy"): "Like Jim Forrestal, Joe McCarthy walked into the Bethesda Naval Hospital as its most controversial patient and as the one man in America most hated by the Communists. And, like Forrestal, he left in a hearse, as a man whose valiant fight against Communism was ended forever."

Going back to Forrestal, the problem with Simpson's theory is that Forrestal's worst enemies were not the Communists, but the Zionists. Although Forrestal's anti-communism later attracted criticism from left-wing historians, it was not, then, a matter of public condemnation. It was his opposition to Zionism, not to Communism, that attracted death threats to Forrestal. In his diary entry for February 3, 1948, Forrestal writes that he mentioned to Bernard Baruch his effort at stopping the process of Israel's recognition: "He took the line of advising me not to be active in this particular matter and that I was already identified, to a degree that was not in my own interests, with opposition to the United Nations policy on Palestine." Martin comments: "Baruch clearly did not know his man when he attempted to influence him by appealing to Forrestal's own self-interest. He might have known more than he was telling, though, when he hinted at the danger that Forrestal faced for the courageous position he had taken."[357]

Jewish gangsters were traditionally anti-communists, but the Zionists could count on them to give a hand whenever needed, as we have seen already. I think it is quite obvious that Forrestal had more to fear from the Zionists than from the Communists. And so it is strange that Simpson totally ignores the Zionists as possible culprits. Neither Israel nor Zionism appears in his index. David Martin finds the explanation for his blackout in the fact that Simpson's book was published by Western Islands Publishers, the in-house publishing company of the John Birch Society, a Zionist front.

Three years before the Birch Society published Simpson's book, Rogow had published the first biography of Forrestal, defending the official line about his death, and linking his supposed mental illness directly to his supposed anti-Semitism. Rogow's focus on anti-Semitism must have led many to consider his book as just another layer in the cover-up. Martin therefore speculates that Simpson's book was a way for the Birch Society to give voice to the skepticism over Forrestal's death, while directing that skepticism away from the most likely suspects. Blaming the Communists was the easiest way to deflect suspicions from the Zionists.

It was all the easier as, in the 1930-50s, Communists and Zionists were often the same people. It is a matter of record that some of the Jews who acted as Communist agents under Roosevelt, turned ardent Zionists under Truman. A case in point is David Niles (Neyhus), one of the few of FDR's top advisors kept by Truman: he was identified in the Venona Decrypts as a Communist agent, but went on playing a key role as a Zionist gatekeeper under Truman. Edwin Wright, in *The Great Zionist Cover-Up,* names him as "the protocol officer in the White House, [who] saw to it that the State Department influence was negated while the Zionist view was presented." David Niles's brother Elliot, a high official of B'nai B'rith, was a Lieutenant Colonel who passed information to the Haganah while working in the Pentagon.

Martin considers David Niles "the most likely coordinator of the Forrestal assassination." He had the motives and the means. He was actually capable of passing orders on behalf of Truman, as he did when orchestrating the campaign of intimidation and corruption that obtained a two-third majority in favor of the Partition Plan at the U.N. General Assembly.[358]

There are reasons to believe that the order to eliminate Forrestal came directly from the White House. Hoopes and Brinkley state that the decision to take Forrestal to Bethesda came from Truman, and that Forrestal's wife was convinced to give her consent by Truman on the phone. The decision to put Forrestal on the 16th floor, which seems hardly appropriate for a suicidal patient, also came from the White House. Hoopes and Brinkley quote Dr. Robert P. Nenno, a young assistant to Dr. Raines from 1952 to 1959, who believed that Raines had received instruction to put Forrestal there, and added, "I have always guessed that the order came from the White House."

Hoopes and Brinkley justify Dr. Raines' turning Sheehy away on six occasions by the fear that Forrestal might divulge sensitive information during confession. Such concerns obviously came from higher up. It didn't come from Navy Secretary John L. Sullivan because, as Hoopes and Brinkley tell us, when Sheehy and Henry Forrestal took their complaint to him on May 18, he expressed surprise and had the decision overruled. According to Simpson: "the priest later commented that he received the distinct impression that Dr. Raines was acting under orders."

There is, of course, no evidence that throwing Forrestal out of the window was also ordered by the White House, but given Truman's complete control by the Zionists, and by David Niles in particular, it makes little difference.

Why kill him after he had been dismissed from power?

But, one may ask, why would Truman or anyone need to kill Forrestal? Once out of the Pentagon, he had no more influence on government policy. The answer is easy. Far from being suicidal, Forrestal was a man with a plan. According to Hoopes and Brinkley, "he had told powerful Wall Street friends . . . that he was interested in starting a newspaper or a magazine modeled after *The*

Economist of Great Britain, and they had demonstrated a willingness to help him raise the start-up funds."

He also planned to write a book. With no more ties to the government or to the army, he was free to speak his mind on many issues. As a war hero and a very popular figure, he was sure to have a great impact. And he had plenty of embarrassing things to reveal about what he had seen during his nine years in the government.

As Navy Secretary, he had been the central person for Pacific operations during World War II. He had inside knowledge of Roosevelt's scheme to provoke the Japanese into attacking Pearl Harbor. According to his diary entry for April 18, 1945, he had even told Truman that, "I had got Admiral Hewitt back to pursue the investigation into the Pearl Harbor disaster. . . . I felt I had an obligation to Congress to continue the investigation because I was not completely satisfied with the report my own Court had made."

Forrestal was also very bitter about the way the war ended in the Pacific. Knowing the desperate situation of the Japanese, he had worked behind the scene to achieve a negotiated surrender from the Japanese. He was opposed to the demand of "unconditional surrender", which he knew was unacceptable to the Japanese military leadership. Simpson writes, as quoted by David Martin:

> As secretary of the navy, Forrestal had originated a plan to end the war with Japan five and a half months before V-J Day finally dawned. He had mapped this plan on the basis of massive intelligence information obtained on and prior to March 1, 1945, to the effect that the Japanese were already desperately anxious to surrender and the fact that the Japanese emperor had even asked the pope to act as peace mediator. If Roosevelt had acted on Forrestal's plan, the war would have ground to a halt in a few days. A-bombs would never have incinerated Hiroshima and Nagasaki, thousands of Americans would not have died in the unnecessary battle of Okinawa and later bloody encounters, and the Russians would not have had a chance to muscle into the Pacific war for the last six of its 1,347 days, thus giving Washington the pretext for handing them the key to the conquest of all Asia.

Forrestal had also much to say about the way the Zionists obtained the Partition Plan at the General Assembly of the United Nations, or about the way Truman was blackmailed and bought into supporting the recognition of Israel. He had written in his diary, February 3, 1948, about his meeting with Franklin D. Roosevelt, Jr., a strong advocate of the Jewish State: "I thought the methods that had been used by people outside of the Executive branch of the government to bring coercion and duress on other nations in the General Assembly bordered closely onto scandal."

Forrestal had a pretty good memory. But, in addition, he had accumulated thousands of pages of diary during his public service. According to Simpson, "During Forrestal's brief stay at Hobe Sound, his personal diaries, consisting of fifteen loose-leaf binders totaling three thousand pages, were hastily removed from his former office in the Pentagon and locked up in the White House where they remained for a year. . . . all during the seven weeks prior to Forrestal's death, his diaries were out of his hands and in the White House, where someone could have had ample time to study them." The White House later claimed that Forrestal had sent word that he wanted President Truman to take custody of these diaries. That is very unlikely.

A small part of Forrestal's diaries was ultimately published in a heavily censored form by Walter Millis, FDR apologist and *New York Herald Tribune* journalist. Simpson estimates that more than 80 percent was left out. Millis frankly admitted that he had deleted unfavorable "references to persons, by name [and] comments reflecting on the honesty or loyalty of an individual." Millis also said that he deleted everything on the Pearl Harbor investigations. One can only guess how much censorship Millis exerted on Forrestal's view about American support for Israel. David Martin's conclusion makes perfect sense:

> Forrestal's writing and publishing plans provide the answer to the question, "Why would anyone bother to murder him when he had already been driven from office and disgraced by the taint of mental illness?" . . . The compelling reasons for Forrestal to want to continue living were also compelling reasons for his powerful enemies to see to it that he did not. . . . He comes across, in short, not as a prime candidate for suicide, but for assassination.[359]

There is a striking parallel between James Forrestal and Joe Kennedy. We remember that in 1941 Joe, very bitter towards Roosevelt, had considered writing his memoirs. He too had still many loyal contacts in the world of the press, including the prestigious *New York Times*. Joe Kennedy, however, preferred to retire from public life and invest his efforts into the future of his children. He thus escaped, personnally, Zionist maliciousness, and, despite the death of his eldest son Joe Jr. in a high-risk mission in 1944, he would achieve through his second son, John, his presidential ambition. The "Kennedy's curse," however, would ultimately catch up with his lineage.

CONCLUSION

"Who cares who killed Kennedy?" once scoffed Noam Chomsky, "I mean, plenty of people die all the time!"[360] How typical! I suspect Chomsky has some idea who killed Kennedy.

Americans and people around the world should care about who killed not just John Kennedy, but his brother Robert too, and probably his son. The Kennedys are important not for who they were as individuals, but for what America lost when she was deprived of their leadership, again and again. The Kennedys are important because an unbiased analysis of their murders exposes the true nature of the power that has enslaved America ever since. A spiritual shadow has descended on America after 1963, extending its darkness over the Western world and beyond, and only the truth about the "Kennedy curse" can begin to lift it.

It is important to educate ourselves and others on the over-whelming evidence incriminating Israel and the traitor Johnson in both Kennedy assassinations. Each Kennedy assassination was an Israeli coup, designed to keep American foreign policy under Zionist control. The assassination of JFK was not only "the crime of the [twentieth] century" — or, as Yuri Slezkine would perhaps say, the "crime of the Jewish century"[361] — it was a Zionist crime, as was the assassination of RFK.

The true story of the Kennedys and their martyrdom has the potential of becoming a new founding myth. Think about the enduring love of millions of Americans for the Kennedys. This love has both a mystical and a patriotic dimension: it is founded on the confused feeling of a hidden truth of existential importance for the nation.

Paradoxically, in a nation founded on the rejection of monarchy, the Kennedys embodied the idea of royalty, a dynastic aristocracy founded not just on the accumulation of wealth and power, but on a patriotic dedication to civil service. It is as if the archetype of royalty has crystallized in the United States on this family, to the point that the name of King Arthur's court, Camelot, has stuck to their legend. The Kennedys also embodied the Irish Catholic root of the American people, with its deep-seated antagonism to British Puritanism, the more Zion-friendly branch of Christianity that has come to dominate American politics.

I admit it: I, too, love the Kennedys. Actually, I adore the Kennedys. Religiously. I think they deserve a heroic cult. "The hero in the Greek religious sense," wrote Lewis Farnell in his classic book on the subject, "is a person whose virtue, influence, or personality was so powerful in his lifetime or through the peculiar circumstances of his death that his spirit after death is regarded as of supernatural power, claiming to be reverenced and propitiated."[362] Religious fervor for heroes, the gratitude we show them and the stories we tell about them, is what binds a people and gives soul to the city.

President John Kennedy and his brother are heroic, almost Christ-like figures in the heart of a community of citizens who are aware of the disastrous longtime effect of their assassinations, and sensitive to the suffocating cover-up imposed from above. The lie is sickening the American psyche, like a repressed family secret affecting many generations from a subconscious level. I firmly believe that only when the American public at large comes to grips with the true nature of "the Kennedy curse", will America have a chance to be redeemed and be great again. The truth will set America free; at least it is a necessary step.

Many Americans understand that the JFK assassination was a coup d'état that stole their country from them, and they are starting to understand who stole it. As if breaking away from a psychopathic bond, they are seeing through the layers of lies that have been piled up over their head. And they are beginning to identify the People of the Lie.

The power of lies must be fought with the power of truth. This is why the Kennedy assassinations are an important battleground. Can you think of a better illustration of Israeli duplicity than Arlen "Magic Bullet" Specter, that "unswerving defender of the Jewish State", titling his autobiography *Passion for Truth*?

Israel doesn't just kill the Kennedys. They keep assassinating their memory, through a constant flow of anti-Kennedy books attacking their character and vilifying their family. This is what JFK researcher James DiEugenio calls "the posthumous assassination of JFK," the obsession to "smother any legacy that might linger"; for "assassination is futile if a man's ideas live on through others."[363] Take for example pseudo-biographer C. David Heymann, who after working for the Mossad in Israel (by his own admission),[364] returned to the U.S.A. only to write Kennedy stories, including the salacious *Bobby and Jackie: A Love Story*. After JFK Jr.'s death, he had the nerves to claim a ten-year secret acquaintance with him, in order to fill the media with rubbish.[365] In a different category, but in the same ethnicity, we have Samuel Halpern, a CIA official who has "made a career of contaminating the Kennedy name," in David Talbot's words. He was Seymour Hersh's key source for his hatchet job, *The Dark Side of Camelot* (1997).[366]

Why so much hatred of the Kennedys from the Chosen Ones? I think I have answered that question.

Why, after almost 60 years, does the lie about Dallas still rule? That is "the deeper question," as Jim DeBrosse correctly points out: "why do JFK conspiracy theories still threaten the powers that be a half century after the assassination? Nearly everyone who might have been involved in a conspiracy is dead and gone. Who, or what, is being protected?"[367] There is obviously a transgenerational dimension to the conspiracy. Is the CIA so powerful as to impose a complete media black-out, not just in America, but in Europe too, for more than half-a-century? Give me a break!

Is the cabal who killed the Kennedys and got away with it still at work today? You bet! Those who control U.S. foreign policy today are the heirs of the assassins of the Kennedys. As Ari Shavit wrote in *Haaretz* in 2003, "The war in Iraq was conceived by 25 neoconservative intellectuals, most of them Jewish, who are pushing President Bush to change the course of history."[368] The crypto-Zionist neoconservatives not only drew the U.S. into the Iraq war under forged intelligence, they are the main designers of the 9/11 false flag attack that has impacted the whole world in a catastrophic way (read my *Unz Review* article "9/11 was an Israeli Job").

Let us try to better understand their vision and their project, because it can shed light on the horrible truth of the "Kennedy curse." The founders of the neoconservative movement were disciples of Leo Strauss, a Jewish immigrant teaching political philosophy at Chicago University. Strauss can be characterized as a secretive, deceitful, Machiavellian, Globo-Zionist. Here is why:

- secretive: In his books, Strauss is notorious for expressing his views only cryptically by attributing them to past philosophers. He shared openly his true philosophy only orally with his close students, who happened to be exclusively Jewish. He took model on Moses Maimonides, whose "secrets," he wrote, "may only be explained in private and only to such individuals as possess both theoretical and political wisdom as well as the capacity of both understanding and using allusive speech." [369]

- deceitful: Strauss believed that national identity can only be sustained in opposition to an enemy, and that the enemy must be mythologized and demonized for public consumption. In several books on Plato, Strauss misused Plato's concept of the "noble lie" (*The Republic*) to endorse the use of mass deception in politics. It is under Strauss's inspiration that Philip Zelikow, before becoming the Executive Director of the 9/11 Commission, specialized in the art of crafting "public myths" by "'searing' or 'molding' events [that] take on 'transcendent' importance and, therefore, retain their power even as the experiencing generation passes from the scene" (his own words, as quoted in Wikipedia).

- Machiavellian: Strauss admired Machiavelli for "the intrepidity of his thought, the grandeur of his vision," and regarded him as the highest patriotic type, because "he is more concerned with the salvation of his fatherland than with the salvation of his soul." For Strauss, only a nation can be eternal, since men have no individual soul; therefore, there is no moral limit to what a (Zionist) patriot can do for his nation. [370] Zionism and Machiavellianism are such twin concepts in the Straussian outlook that Strauss's disciple Michael Ledeen hypothesized that

Machiavelli was as secret Jew: "Listen to his political philosophy, and you will hear the Jewish music."[371]

- Globo-Zionist: Strauss was an ardent (yet discreet) supporter of the State of Israel, but also believed that Jews must continue to be a nation dispersed among other nations, particularly in the United States. In a 1962 lecture at the Hillel Foundation, "Why We Remain Jews", he quoted, as "the most profound and radical statement on assimilation that I have read", Nietzsche's *Dawn of Day* aphorism 205, which predicts that the Jews will become "the lords of Europe": "at some time Europe may fall like a perfectly ripe fruit into their hand, which only casually reaches out. In the meantime it is necessary for them to distinguish themselves in all the areas of European distinction and to stand among the first, until they will be far enough along to determine themselves that which distinguishes."[372] Replace "Europe" by "the West", and you have the Straussian agenda.

Is Strauss's Machiavellian crypto-Zionism a Jewish aberration? No. Before Netanyahu and the neocon gang, there was Ben-Gurion and the Feinberg gang. Same philosophy, same method: treachery and deception, for the purpose of pulling the U.S. into proxy wars for Israel. Same vision: Jewish supremacism. In 1962, the same year as Strauss's lecture "Why We Remain Jews," Ben-Gurion predicted in the magazine *Look* that, within 25 years, Jerusalem "will be the seat of the Supreme Court of Mankind, to settle all controversies among the federated continents, as prophesied by Isaiah."[373] Indeed, Isaiah prophesied: "For the Law will issue from Zion and the word of Yahweh from Jerusalem. Then he will judge between the nations and arbitrate between many peoples" (2:3-4). In other words, Israel will rule the world. The political vision of Ben-Gurion, as of most Israeli leaders after him, is steeped in the Hebrew Bible. "There can be no worthwhile political or military education about Israel without profound knowledge of the Bible," he said.[374] Ben-Gurion's standard biography by Dan Kurzman, titled *Prophet of Fire,* portrays him as Moses, Joshua, and Isaiah, with a biblical quote for each chapter's title.

Isaiah, the Zionists' favorite prophet, also said: "the nation and kingdom that will not serve you will perish, and . . . will be utterly destroyed" (60:12); "You will suck the milk of nations, you will suck the wealth of kings" (60:16); "You will feed on the wealth of nations, you will supplant them in their glory" (61:6).

This is the biblical blueprint of the Zionist World Order, promised by Israel's jealous god in Deuteronomy: "devour all the peoples whom Yahweh your god puts at your mercy, show them no pity" (7:16); "he will raise you higher than every other nation he has made" (28:1); "You will make many nations your subjects, yet you will be subject to none" (28:12).

It takes a free-thinker like H. G. Wells to see it for what it is: "a conspiracy against the rest of the world." In the books of the Bible, "you have the conspiracy plain and clear, . . . an aggressive and vindictive conspiracy. . . . It is not tolerance but stupidity to shut our eyes to their quality."[375]

Watch the film based on this research, and share it:
"Assassination of the Kennedy Brothers"
on https://odysee.com/@KontreKulture:c/Israel-and-the-
Assassinations-of-The-Kennedy-brothers:9

contact the author at l.guyenot109@orange.fr

NOTES

Introduction

1. Quoted in Michael Collins Piper, *Final Judgment: The Missing Link in the JFK Assassination Conspiracy,* American Free Press, 6th ed., 2005, p. 63.
2. I have used the sixth edition published in 2005, available on archive.org. Following Piper's footsteps means that I started by walking backward the trail of his bibliography and his endnotes. As a rule, in my own endnotes, I do not reference Piper's book when I have consulted his sources directly. Consequently, my notes do not reflect the amount of information I borrowed from him. But readers who are familiar with his work will easily recognize my debt.
3. Lance deHaven-Smith, *Conspiracy Theory in America*, University of Texas Press, 2013, kindle l. 284-292.
4. Arthur Krock, *Memoirs: Sixty Years on the Firing Line*, Funk & Wagnalls, 1968, p. 328.

Chapter 1: RFK's false-flag assassination

5. Benjamin Bradlee, *Conversations with Kennedy,* W.W. Norton, 1975, p. 138.
6. Laurence Leamer, *Sons of Camelot: The Fate of an American Dynasty,* HarperCollins, 2005, kindle l. 225.
7. Associated Press, "RFK children speak about JFK assassination," January 12, 2013, on www.usatoday.com
8. David Talbot, *Brothers: The Hidden History of the Kennedy Years,* Simon & Schuster, 2007, pp. 278-280, 305.
9. Talbot, *Brothers,* pp. 25-27.
10. Talbot, *Brothers*, pp. 21-22.
11. Leamer, *Sons of Camelot,* l. 465.
12. James Hepburn, *Farewell America: The Plot to Kill JFK,* Penmarin Books, 2002, p. 269.
13. Talbot, *Brothers,* pp. 312-314. Frank Mankiewicz told David Talbot that in 1967 Robert had privately asked him to keep him informed about Garrison's investigation, but that Robert "couldn't focus" when he shared his view that "there was some sort of conspiracy, probably involving the mob, anti-Castro Cuban exiles, and maybe rogue CIA agents" (Talbot, *Brothers,* p. 312). I regard this self-serving statement as worthless.
14. Talbot, *Brothers,* p. 333.
15. Watch in *Evidence of Revision: Part 4: The RFK assassination as never seen before*, 01:11:42
16. Jerry Cohen, "Yorty Reveals That Suspect's Memo Set Deadline for Death," *Los Angeles Times,* June 6, 1968, on latimesblogs.latimes.com; Jerry Cohen, "Jerusalem-Born Suspect Called An Anti-Semite," *The Salt Lake Tribune*, June 6, 1968, read on www.newspapers.com but no longer available.
17. Tim Tate and Brad Johnson, *The Assassination of Robert F. Kennedy: Crime Conspiracy & Cover-Up: A new investigation* (2018), 2nd edition, Lume Books, 2020, p. 87.

18. Jeffrey Salkin, "Remember What Bobby Kennedy Died For," *Forward.com,* June 5, 2008. Also Michael Fischbach, "First Shot in Terror War Killed RFK," *Los Angeles Times,* June 02, 2003, on articles.latimes.com

19. Sasha Issenberg, "Slaying gave US a first taste of Mideast terror," *Boston Globe,* June 5, 2008, on www.boston.com

20. First discovered in 1970 by Pasadena criminologist William Harper. John Crewdson, "6 Years Later, Evidence in Sirhan's Case Is Questioned," *New York Times,* December 15, 1974, on www.nytimes.com

21. Tate and Johnson, *The Assassination of Robert F. Kennedy,* pp. 184-203 (196); Frank Morales, "The Assassination of RFK: A Time for Justice!" June 16, 2012, on www.globalresearch.ca; watch "RFK Assassination 40th Anniversary (2008) Paul Schrade on CNN" on YouTube.

22. "Robert F Kennedy's killer loses 15th parole bid as witness says: 'It's my fault'", Feb 11, 2016, on www.thegardian.com

23. Stephanie Haney "Bobby Kennedy's children at war with each other over new death probe," June 2, 2018, on dailymail.com

24. Watch Ted Charach and Gerald Alcan's film *The Second Gun: Who Really Killed Robert Kennedy,* 1998, on YouTube.

25. Philip Melanson, *The Robert F. Kennedy Assassination: New Revelations On the Conspiracy And Cover-Up,* S.P.I. Books, 1994, p. 25. On Cesar, also Tate and Johnson, *The Assassination of Robert F. Kennedy,* pp. 225-244.

26. William Klaber and Philip Melanson, *Shadow Play: The Unsolved Murder of Robert F. Kennedy,* (first ed. 1997), Macmillan, 2018, pp. 116-134. Brad Johnson has come with a plausible identification of the girl in the polka dot dress, as being Elayn Neal, whose second husband, Jerry Capehart, told his son that he had worked in mind control experiment for the CIA: Tate and Johnson, *The Assassination of Robert F. Kennedy,* pp. 245-292.

27. Klaber and Melanson, *Shadow Play,* pp. 6-7, 65.

28. In a parole hearing in 2011. Watch "Sirhan Sirhan Denied Parole" on YouTube.

29. Shane O'Sullivan, *Who Killed Bobby? The Unsolved Murder of Robert F. Kennedy*, Union Square Press, 2008, pp. 5, 44, 103.

30. Klaber and Melanson, *Shadow Play,* pp. 197, 199.

31. In Shane O'Sullivan's 2007 documentary *RFK Must Die: The Assassination of Bobby Kennedy,* on YouTube.

32. On Dr. Brown's tests, read Tate and Johnson, *The Assassination of Robert F. Kennedy*, pp. 313-335.

33. Tate and Johnson, *The Assassination of Robert F. Kennedy*, pp. 105, 108.

34. William Turner and John Christian, *The Assassination of Robert F. Kennedy: The Conspiracy and Cover-up* (1978), Basic Books, 2006, pp. 225-229.

35. Colin Ross, *Bluebird: Deliberate Creation of Multiple Personality by Psychiatrists*, Manitou Communications, 2000, summary on www.wanttoknow.info/bluebird10pg

36. Larry Romanoff, "CIA Project MK-Ultra," on www.unz.com

37. Ronen Bergman, *Rise and Kill First: The Secret History of Israel's Targeted Assassinations*, Random House, 2018, pp. 117-119.

38. Alexander Cockburn, ed., *The Politics of Anti-Semitism,* AK Press, 2003, p. 104.

39. Victor Ostrovsky, *The Other Side of Deception: A Rogue Agent Exposes the Mossad's Secret Agenda,* HarperCollins, 1994.

40. Rowan Scarborough, "U.S. troops would enforce peace Under Army study," *The Washington Times,* 10 septembre 2001, on www.washingtontimes.com

41. Gordon Thomas, *Gideon's Spies: The Secret History of the Mossad,* St. Martin's Press, 1999, pp. 384-385, 410-411.

42. Piper, *Final Judgment,* pp. 343, 347.

43. Frank Mankiewicz, *So As I Was Saying... My Somewhat Eventful Life,* with Joel Swerdlow, MacMillan, 2016, p. 10.

44. Ron Unz, "American Pravda: The ADL in American Society," October 15, 2018, on unz.com.

45. David Lawrence, "Paradoxical Bob," *Independent Star-News,* May 26, 1968, page 14, on www.newspapers.com/; Shane O'Sullivan, *RFK Must Die,* on YouTube, at 00:14.

46. Arthur Krock, *Memoirs: Sixty Years on the Firing Line,* Funk & Wagnalls, 1968, p. 347.

47. The Israel Lobby Archive, www.irmep.org/ila/forrel/

48. Klaber and Melanson, *Shadow Play,* p. 160.

49. Salkin, "Remember What Bobby Kennedy Died For."

50. Judy Maltz, "Bobby Kennedy's Little-known Visit to the Holy Land That Made Him pro-Israel – and Got Him Killed," *The Forward,* June 8, 2018, on www.haaretz.com/

51. Klaber and Melanson, *Shadow Play,* pp. 116-134.

Chapter 2: JFK and the Samson Option

52. Tim Tate and Brad Johnson, *The Assassination of Robert F. Kennedy: Crime Conspiracy & Cover-Up: A new investigation* (2018), 2nd edition Lume Books, 2020, p. 293.

53. Michael Collins Piper, *False Flags: Template for Terror,* American Free Press, 2013, p. 67.

54. Meir Doron, *Confidential: The Life of Secret Agent Turned Hollywood Tycoon - Arnon Milchan,* Gefen Books, 2011, p. xi.

55. Stuart Winer, "Hollywood producer Arnon Milchan reveals past as secret agent," November 25, 2013, on www.timesofisrael.com

56. Philip Muehlenbeck, *Betting on the Africans: John F. Kennedy's Courting of African Nationalist Leaders,* Oxford UP, 2012, pp. 122-124.

57. George and Douglas Ball, *The Passionate Attachment: America's Involvement With Israel, 1947 to the Present,* W.W. Norton & Co., 1992, p. 51.

58. Michael Collins Piper, *Final Judgment: The Missing Link in the JFK Assassination Conspiracy,* American Free Press, 6th ed., 2005, p. 115.

59. Stephen Green, *Taking Sides,* p. 251.

60. Seymour Hersh, *The Samson Option: Israel's Nuclear Arsenal and American Foreign Policy,* Random House, 1991, pp. 93, 97.

61. Arthur Schlesinger Jr, *Journals: 1952-2000,* Penguin Books, 2008, p. 96.

62. James Douglass, *JFK and the Unspeakable: Why He Died and Why It Matters,* Touchstone, 2008, pp. 151-152, 163-167, 190-192, 197-202.

63. The Israel Lobby Archive, www.irmep.org/ila/forrel/

64. Fulbright on CBS, April 15, 1973, quoted in Jeff Gates, *Guilt by Association: How Deception and Self-Deceit Took American to War,* State Street Publications, 2008.

65. Alan Hart, *Zionism: The Real Enemy of the Jews,* vol. 2: *David Becomes Goliath,* Clarity Press, 2009, p. 273.

66. JFK Library: www.jfklibrary.org/Asset-Viewer/DOPIN64xJUGRKgdHJ9NfgQ.aspx
67. JFK Library : www.jfklibrary.org/Asset-Viewer/ZNOo49DpRUa-kMetjWmSyg.aspx
68. Ted Sorensen, *Kennedy* (1965), Harper Perennial, 2009, p. 740.
69. Audio file on JFK Library: www.jfklibrary.org/learn/about-jfk/historic-speeches/televised-address-on-nuclear-test-ban-treaty
70. Audio file on JFK Library: www.jfklibrary.org/Asset-Viewer/Archives/JFKWHA-169.aspx
71. Avner Cohen, *Israel and the Bomb,* Columbia UP, 1998, pp. 10-13.
72. Avner Cohen, quoted in Jefferson Morley, *The Ghost: The Secret Life of CIA Spymaster James Jesus Angleton,* St. Martin's Press, 2017, p. 175.
73. Ted Snider, "Israel-linked assassinations: How much is the US really involved?", December 21, 2020, on responsiblestatecraft.org
74. Cohen, *Israel and the Bomb,* pp. 91, 107.
75. "Kennedy-Ben-Gurion Meeting (May 30, 1961)," on www.jewishvirtuallibrary.org/
76. Hersh, *The Samson Option,* p. 111.
77. Hersh, *The Samson Option,* p. 117.
78. Cohen, *Israel and the Bomb*, pp. 109 and 14; Hersh, *The Samson Option,* p. 121.
79. Cohen, *Israel and the Bomb,* p. 129.
80. Cohen, *Israel and the Bomb,* pp. 128-134; Warren Bass, *Support any Friend: Kennedy's Middle East and the Making of the U.S.-Israel Alliance,* 2003, p. 219.
81. Cohen, *Israel and the Bomb*, p. 13.
82. Cohen, *Israel and the Bomb,* pp. 154-155.
83. Harry S. Traynor, Atomic Energy Commission representative to U.S. Intelligence Board, "Report on U.S. Inspection team Visit to Dimona, Israel," 30 January 1964, Secret, on nsarchive.gwu.edu/
84. Review by Reuven Pedatzur on *Haaretz*, Feb. 5, 1999, quoted in Michael Collins Piper, *False Flags: Template for Terror,* American Free Press, 2013, pp. 54–55.
85. "Gaddafi Speech 2008 – Israel Assassinated Kennedy!" on YouTube, or with video in our film "Assassinations of the Kennedy Brothers," on YouTube at 59 min.
86 "Muammar Gaddafi speech at the United Nations, on 23/9/2012" on libyanfreepress.wordpress.com/
87. Joe Sterling, "Jewish paper's column catches Secret Service's eye," CNN, January 22, 2012.
88. Bryan Edward Stone, *The Chosen Folks: Jews on the Frontiers of Texas,* University of Texas Press, 2010, p. 200.
89. That has first been proposed by Harold Weisberg in *Whitewash,* Dell Publishing, 1966.
90. Article reproduced by Jim Phelps on educationforum
91. John Hughes-Wilson, *JFK-An American Coup d'État: The Truth Behind the Kennedy Assassination,* John Blake, 2014.
92. Natasha Mozgovaya, "Prominent Jewish-American politician Arlen Specter dies at 82," *Haaretz,* October 14, 2012, on www.haaretz.com.

Chapter 3: LBJ, Israel's Best Friend

93. Stephen Green, *Taking Sides: America's Secret Relations With a Militant Israel,* William Morrow & Co., 1984, p. 166.

94. Avner Cohen and William Burr, "How Israel Built a Nuclear Program Right Under the Americans' Noses," January 17, 2021 on www.haaretz.com/

95. Green, *Taking Sides,* p. 251.

96. Ron Kampeas, "Lyndon Johnson: Israel Has Had No Better Friend," *Haaretz,* May 9, 2018, on www.haaretz.com/

97. Andrew and Leslie Cockburn, *Dangerous Liaison: The Inside Story of the U.S.-Israeli Covert Relationship,* HarperCollins, 1991, pp. 140-147.

98. Letter From President Johnson to Prime Minister Eshkol, Washington, June 3, 1967, on history.state.gov.

99. Phillip F. Nelson, *LBJ: From Mastermind to "The Colossus",* Skyhorse, 2014, kindle pp. 501-503, 511, quoting Nicholas, Katzenbach, *Some of It Was Fun: Working With JFK and LBJ,* W.W. Norton & Co., 2008, pp. 251-252, and Joseph Califano, Jr., *The Triumph and Tragedy of Lyndon Johnson,* Simon & Shuster, 1991, p. 204.

100. Robert Allen, *Beyond Treason: Reflections on the Cover-up of the June 1967 Israeli Attack on the USS Liberty, an American Spy Ship,* CreateSpace, 2012.

101. As told by Lt. Commander David Lewis, who received this testimony from Geis, with the caution: "What I'm about to tell you is for your ears only, you're not to tell anyone during my lifetime." Also in Mellen, *Blood in the Water,* p. 182.

102. Joan Mellen, *Blood in the Water: How the US and Israel Conspired to Ambush the USS Liberty,* Prometheus Books, 2018 (on www.worldtruth.online), p. 177.

103. Mellen, *Blood in the Water,* p. 235.

104. Kampeas, "Lyndon Johnson: Israel Has Had No Better Friend."

105. Buy or rent the film at www.sacrificingliberty.com/watch

106. George and Douglas Ball, *The Passionate Attachment: America's Involvement With Israel, 1947 to the Present,* WW Norton & Co, 1992.

107. Robert Allen, *Beyond Treason: Reflections on the Cover-up of the June 1967 Israeli Attack on the USS Liberty, an American Spy Ship,* CreateSpace, 2012.

108. As best captured by Greg Felton in *The Host and the Parasite: How Israel's Fifth Column Consumed America,* Bad Bear Press, 2012.

109. Mellen, *Blood in the Water,* p. 32.

110. Nelson, *LBJ: From Mastermind to "The Colossus",* kindle p. 511.

111. Morris Smith, "Our First Jewish President Lyndon Johnson? – an update!!," *5 Towns Jewish Times,* April 11, 2013, taken off 5tjt.com but saved on web.archive.org

112. Seymour Hersh, *The Samson Option: Israel's Nuclear Arsenal and American Foreign Policy*, Random House, 1991, p. 127.

113. LBJ Library, quoted in Phillip F. Nelson, *LBJ: From Mastermind to "The Colossus",* Skyhorse, 2014, kindle p. 281.

114. "Letter from Senator Lyndon B. Johnson o the Secretary of State," February 11, 1957, on history.state.gov/historicaldocuments/frus1955-57v17/d83

115. Hersh, *The Samson Option,* p. 192.

116. Quoted in Nelson, *LBJ: From Mastermind to "The Colossus",* kindle p. 286.

117. Robert McNamara, *In Retrospect: The Tragedy and Lessons of Vietnam,* Times Books, 1995, p. 96.

118. Howard Jones, *Death of a Generation: How the Assassinations of Diem and JFK Prolonged the Vietnam War,* Oxford UP, 2003. Listen to a one-hour lecture by Howard Jones for the National Archives on www.c-span.org

119. On JFK Library, www.jfklibrary.org

120. James Douglass, *JFK and the Unspeakable: Why He Died and Why It Matters,* Touchstone, 2008, pp. 107, 102. Close collaborators who quote Kennedy expressing

his firm determination not to send troops include Malcolm Kilduff, Tip O'Neill, Kenneth O'Donnell, David Powers, and many more.

121. On www.discoverlbj.org/item/nsf-nsam273

122. On www.discoverlbj.org/item/nsf-nsam288

123. *Seven Days in May* is a political thriller published in 1962, about a military coup for control of the White House. See Douglass, *JFK and the Unspeakable,* pp. 186 and 196.

124. Douglass, *JFK and the Unspeakable,* p. 15.

125. It may be objected that, according to Krock, his friendship with JFK "broke apart" some months earlier (*Memoirs: Sixty Years on the Firing Line*, Funk & Wagnalls, 1968, p. 358). Krock gives no explanation, but Kennedy told his friend Ben Bradlee, that "Krock had never forgiven him for the *Newsweek* story on the Washington press corps, in which I had quoted the president as saying that he no longer read Krock" (Benjamin Bradlee, *Conversations with Kennedy,* W.W. Norton, 1975, p. 132).

126. Tom Wicker, *JFK and LBJ: The Influence of Personality Upon Politics,* William Morrow, 1968, p. 185.

127. Fletcher Prouty, *The CIA, Vietnam, and the Plot to Assassinat John F. Kennedy,* Skyhorse Publishing, 2011.

128. Joan Mellen, *A Farewell to Justice,* Potomac Books, 2007.

129. According to Arthur Goldberg, as quoted in Robert Dallek, *Flawed Giant: Lyndon Johnson and His Times, 1961-1973,* Oxford UP, 1998, p. 491.

130. David Halberstam, *The Best and the Brightest,* Random House, 1972, p. 762.

131. John K. Galbraith, "Exit Strategy – In 1963, JFK ordered a complete withdrawal from Vietnam," Oct/Nov 2003, on bostonreview.net ;

132. *Breaking Ranks,* 1979, quoted in Philip Weiss, "Journalists Refuse to Weigh Neocons' Own Statements of Israel-Centered Foreign Policy," April 24, 2007, on *Mondoweiss.net.*

133. Film of De Gaulle's press conference on fresques.ina.fr/ at 41 min.

134. Jean Lacouture, *De Gaulle : Tome 3, le souverain (1959-1970),* Seuil, 2010, p. 507.

135. On the Jewish-led student uprising in Paris in 1968, read Yair Auron, *Les Juifs d'extrême gauche en Mai 68,* Albin Michel, 1998.

136. Rabbi Moshe Shonfeld, *Holocaust Victims Accuse: Documents and Testimony of Jewish War Criminals*, Bnei Yeshivos, 1977, on netureikartaru.com, pp. 28, 24.

137. Kenneth O'Donnell and David Powers, *"Johnny We Hardly Knew Ye": Memories of John Fitzgerald Kennedy*, Litle, Brown and Co., 1970, pp. 182-200 (p. 193). Johnson of course saw things differently: to Clare Boothe Luce, who asked him why he had accepted a post clearly less strategic than Majority Leader in the Senate, which he held prior to his nomination, he replied: "One out of every four presidents has died in office. I'm a gamblin' man, darlin', and this is the only chance I got." Richard Mahoney, *The Kennedy Brothers: The Rise and Fall of Jack and Bobby,* Arcade Publishing, 2011, p. 64.

138. Seymour Hersh, *The Dark Side of Camelot,* Little, Brown & Co, 1997, p. 126, quoted in Phillip Nelson, *LBJ: The Mastermind of JFK's Assassination,* XLibris, 2010, p. 320.

139. Kenneth O'Donnell and David Powers, *"Johnny We Hardly Knew Ye": Memories of John Fitzgerald Kennedy*, Litle, Brown and Co., 1970, pp. 193, 200.

140. Pierre Salinger, *With Kennedy,* Garden City, 1966, p. 57.

141. Arthur Schlesinger, *A Thousand Days: John Kennedy in the White House* (1965), Mariner Books, 2002, p. 56.

142. Alan Hart, *Zionism, the Real Enemy of the Jews,* vol. 2: *David Becomes Goliath,* Clarity Press, 2009, p. 257.

143. Deborah Davis, *Katharine the Great,* Harcourt Brace Jovanovich, 1979, p. 249.

144. Eddie Fisher, *Been there, done that,* St. Martin's Press, 1999, p. 258.

145. Jacqueline Kennedy, *Historic Conversations on Life with John F. Kennedy,* Hyperion, 2011.

146. Jeff Shesol, *Mutual Contempt: Lyndon Johnson, Robert Kennedy, and the Feud that Defined a Decade,* WW Norton & Co, 1997, 2012, p. 95.

147. Madeleine Brown, *Texas in the Morning,* 1997, p. 167, quoted in Phillip Nelson, *LBJ: The Mastermind of JFK's Assassination,* XLibris, 2010, p. 376.

148. William Reymond and Billie Sol Estes, *JFK. Le Dernier témoin,* Flammarion, 2003.

149 The tabloid *National Enquire* has also popularized the theory, most recently in its December 2, 2019 issue, with the headline: "New evidence shows LBJ ordered killing of JFK!"

150. Quoted in Phillip Nelson, *LBJ: The Mastermind of JFK's Assassination,* XLibris, 2010, p. 17.

151. Nelson, *LBJ: The Mastermind,* p. 370.

152. Article "Don B. Reynolds" on spartacus-educational.com/ Copy of the FBI report on www.maryferrell.org/

153. Evelyn Lincoln, *Kennedy and Johnson,* 1968, Holt, Rinehart and Winston, pp. 200, 204-205. Kennedy aides Kenneth O'Donnell and David Powers contradict her (*"Johnny, We Hardly Knew Ye",* p. 5). But O'Donnell and Powers have very carefully purged their narrative of anything that might shed doubt on the Warren Commission's conclusion.

154. "Nixon jokes about LBJ killing JFK," on YouTube.

155. Patrick Howley, "Why Jack Ruby was probably part of the Kennedy conspiracy," *The Daily Caller,* March 14, 2014, on dailycaller.com

156. Copy on jfkmurdersolved.com. The forgery is proven by several inconsistencies: first, Nixon was a freshman in the role as junior counsel in 1947, and only started prosecuting Alger Hiss (the only likely context for this memo) the next year. Secondly, it refers to "Jack Rubenstein" living in Chicago in November of 1947, when Ruby had in fact already changed his name and moved to Dallas by that time. Finally, the document carries a zip code when they did not exist at the time.

157. This sequence can be seen in the 1988 documentary "The day the dream died" at 38:20; for more information on Ruby's declarations about Johnson and about Jews, check on jfkmurdersolved.com.

158. Read Ruby's deposition is on jfkmurdersolved.com

159. Seth Kantor, *The Ruby Cover-Up,* Zebra Books, 1980, p. 49.

160. Transcript on mcadams.posc.mu.edu

161. Nelson, *LBJ: The Mastermind,* p. 604-7. Letter reproduced on mcadams.posc.mu.edu

162. Charles A. Crenshaw, *JFK, Conspiracy of Silence,* Signet, 1992, pp. 185-189.

Chapter 4: Jack Ruby, Gangster for Zion

163. Seth Kantor, *The Ruby Cover-Up,* Zebra Books, 1980, p. 49.

164. Steve North, "Lee Harvey Oswald's Killer 'Jack Ruby' Came From Strong Jewish Background," *The Forward,* November 17, 2013, on forward.com

165. William Kunstler, *My Life as a Radical Lawyer,* Carol Publishing, 1994, p. 158.

166. James Douglass, *JFK and the Unspeakable: Why He Died and Why It Matters,* Touchstone, 2008, p. 357.
167. Douglass, *JFK and the Unspeakable,* p. 47 ; Sheriff's Office report on mcadams.posc.mu.edu/death2.txt
168. Jim Marrs, *Crossfire: The Plot that Killed Kennedy,* Carroll and Graf, 1989, p. 285.
169. Douglass, *JFK and the Unspeakable,* pp. 169-171.
170. On https://mcadams.posc.mu.edu/russ/testimony/paine_r3.htm
171. Seth Kantor, *The Ruby Cover-up,* Zebra Books, 1980, p. 48.
172. en.wikipedia.org/wiki/Jack_Ruby - Ruby's_motive
173. Gaeton Fonzi, *The Last Investigation: A Former Federal Investigator Reveals the Man Behind the Conspiracy to Kill JFK,* 1993, Skyhorse, 2013, kindle l. 405–76.
174. Michael Collins Piper, *Final Judgment: The Missing Link in the JFK Assassination Conspiracy,* American Free Press, 6th ed., 2005, p. 239.
175. Hank Messick, *Lansky,* Putnam's Sons, 1971, p. 9.
176. Michael Collins Piper, *Final Judgment,* p. 222.
177. Gary Wean, *There's a Fish in the Courthouse,* Casitas Books, 1987, p. 681, quoted by Piper, *Final Judgment,* p. 219-27, 232-7.
178. Piper, *Final Judgment,* p. 224.
179. Read more on www.israellobby.org/Feinberg/default.asp
180. Read Ricky-Dale Calhoun, "Arming David: The Haganah's illegal arms procurement network in the United States 1945-1949," *Journal of Palestine Studies* Vol. XXXVI, No. 4 (Summer 2007), pp. 22–32, on www.ampalestine.org.
181. Robert Rockaway, "Gangsters for Zion. Yom Ha'atzmaut: How Jewish mobsters helped Israel gain its independence", April 19, 2018, on tabletmag.com
182. Alan J. Weberman and Michael Canfield, *Coup d'État in America: The CIA and the Assassination of John F. Kennedy,* Quick American Archives, 1975, pp. 151-180 (p. 178). Michael Collins Piper mentions (*Final Judgment,* p. 232) that Weberman has revealed that Ruby traveled to Israel in 1955, but the link to Weberman's website is now dead, and I hold Weberman as an unreliable source.
183. Bernard Fensterwald, *Coincidence or Conspiracy,* 1977, quoted by Piper, *Final Judgment,* pp. 228-229.
184. Richard Gildbride, *Matrix for Assassination: the JFK Conspiracy,* Trafford, 2009.
185. Kantor, *The Ruby Cover-Up,* pp. 255-264, 402.
186. Kantor, *The Ruby Cover-Up,* p. 48.
187. Kantor, *The Ruby Cover-Up,* p. 53.
188. Kantor, *The Ruby Cover-Up,* pp. 56-59.
189. Kantor, *The Ruby Cover-Up,* p. 91.
190. John Hughes-Wilson, *JFK-An American Coup d'État: The Truth Behind the Kennedy Assassination,* John Blake, 2014.
191. "Ruby's murder of Oswald was premeditated," on Youtube.
192. Kantor, *The Ruby Cover-Up,* pp. 96-97.
193. Deposition online on mcadams.posc.mu.edu/russ/testimony/eberhard.htm
194. Kantor, *The Ruby Cover-Up,* p. 98.
195. Photo on www.loc.gov/item/2003672755/
196. Kantor, *The Ruby Cover-Up,* pp. 100-101.
197. Kantor, *The Ruby Cover-Up,* p. 116.
198. Kantor, *The Ruby Cover-Up,* p. 132.
199. Kantor, *The Ruby Cover-Up,* pp. 141, 409.

200. Jefferson Morley, "Ex-flame says Jack Ruby had no choice but to kill Oswald", Aug. 20, 2019, on jfkfacts.org/

201. Watch his interview two hours after JFK's assassination in the History Channel documentary *JFK - 3 Shots That Changed America*, at 43:34.

202. Michael L. Kurtz, *The JFK Assassination Debates: Lone Gunman versus Conspiracy*, University Press of Kansas, 2006, p. 47.

203. Douglass, *JFK and the Unspeakable*, p. 361.

Chapter 5: Jim Angleton, Mossad's CIA Asset

204. Jefferson Morley, *Our Man in Mexico: Winston Scott and the Hidden History of the CIA*, University Press of Kansas, 2008, p. 207.

205 . Morley, *Our Man in Mexico*, p. 212.

206. James Douglass, *JFK and the Unspeakable: Why He Died and Why It Matters*, Touchstone, 2008, pp. 75-81, 228-233.

207. Douglass, *JFK and the Unspeakable*, pp. 81 and 232.

208. Douglass, *JFK and the Unspeakable*, pp. 82-83.

209. "LBJ speaks on a conspiracy in JFK murder," on YouTube.

210. John M. Newman, *Oswald and the CIA: The Documented Truth About the Unknown Relationship Between the U.S. Government and the Alleged Killer of JFK*, Skyhorse, 2008, pp. 613-637. Excerpts on spartacus-educational.com

211. Peter Dale Scott, *Deep Politics and the Death of JFK*, University of California Press, 1993, pp. 38-44.

212. Newman, *Oswald and the CIA*, pp. 636-637 (on spartacus-educational.com)

213. Douglass, *JFK and the Unspeakable*, p. 144.

214. On Scott and Phillips's connections to Angleton, read Jefferson Morley, *Our Man in Mexico: Winston Scott and the Hidden History of the CIA*, University Press of Kansas, 2008.

215. Jefferson Morley, *The Ghost: The Secret Life of CIA Spymaster James Jesus Angleton*, St. Martin's Press, 2017, pp. 130-132.

216. I have not consulted directly Michael Holzman, *James Jesus Angleton, the CIA and the Craft of Counterintelligence*, University of Massachusetts Press, 2008.

217. Tom Mangold, *Cold Warrior: James Jesus Angleton: the CIA's Master Spy Hunter*, Simon & Schuster, 1991, p. 52.

218. Morley, *The Ghost*, p. 106.

219 Mangold, *Cold Warrior*, p. 55.

220. Andrew and Leslie Cockburn, *Dangerous Liaison: The Inside Story of the U.S.-Israeli Covert Relationship*, HarperCollins, 1991, p. 43.

221. Mangold, *Cold Warrior*, p. 57.

222. Morley, *The Ghost*, p. 229.

223. David C. Martin, *Wilderness of Mirrors: Intrigue, Deception, and the Secrets that Destroyed Two of the Cold War's Most Important Agents*, Skyhorse, 2018, p. 201.

224. David Wise, "The Spookiest of the CIA's Spooks," *Los Angeles Times*, December 24, 2006, on www.latimes.com. Colby is also quoted in Tennent H. Bably, *Spy Wars: Moles, Mysteries, and Deadly Games*, Yale UP, 2007, p. 214.

225. Jefferson Morley, "Wilderness of Mirrors: Documents Reveal the Complex "Legacy of James Angleton, CIA Counterintelligence Chief and Godfather of Mass Surveillance", January 1, 2018, *The Intercept*, on theintercept.com/

226. Peter Dale Scott, *Deep Politics and the Death of JFK,* University of California Press, 1993, p. 54, quoted in Michael Collins Piper, *Final Judgment: The Missing Link in the JFK Assassination Conspiracy,* American Free Press, 6th ed., 2005, p. 63.
227. Morley, *The Ghost,* pp. 106, 70.
228. Mangold, *Cold Warrior,* p. 362.
229. Mangold, *Cold Warrior,* p. 49.
230. Cockburn and Cockburn, *Dangerous Liaison,* p. 41.
231. Morley, *The Ghost,* 55
232. Cockburn, *Dangerous Liaison,* p. 43.
233. Cockburn, *Dangerous Liaison,* p. 65; Morley, *The Ghost,* p. 78.
234. Morley, *The Ghost,* p. 171.
235. Morley, *The Ghost,* pp. 174, 73; Jefferson Morley, "Wilderness of Mirrors."
236. Morley, *The Ghost,* p. 262.
237. Jefferson Morley, "CIA and Mossad: Tradeoffs in the Formation of the U.S.-Israel Strategic Relationship," conf for the Washington Report on Middle East Affairs, 2018 May, on www.wrmea.org/
238. Morley, *The Ghost,* p. 174.
239. Seymour Hersh, *The Samson Option: Israel's Nuclear Arsenal and American Foreign Policy*, Random House, 1991, p. 147.
240. Morley, *The Ghost,* p. 92
241. Morley, "CIA and Mossad."
242. Morley, *The Ghost,* pp. 261-262.
243. Michael Holzman, *James Jesus Angleton: The CIA, and the Craft of Counterintelligence,* University of Massachusetts Press, 2008, pp. 167-168.
244. Cockburn, *Dangerous Liaison,* pp. 146-147.
245. Joan Mellen, *Blood in the Water: How the US and Israel Conspired to Ambush the USS Liberty,* Prometheus Books, 2018, on www.worldtruth.online/, p. 50.
246. Peter Hounam, *Operation Cyanide: Why the Bombing of the USS Liberty nearly caused World War III,* Vision, 2003, pp. 266-267.
247. Mellen, *Blood in the Water*, pp. 37-40.
248. Mellen, *Blood in the Water,* p. 49.
249. Tom Segev, *1967: Israel, the War, and the Year That Transformed the Middle East,* Henry Hold, 2007, pp. 329-332.
250. Morley, "CIA and Mossad"
251. Glenn Frankel, "The Secret Ceremony," *Washington Post,* December 5, 1987, on www.washingtonpost.com. Andy Court's article, "Spy Chiefs Honour a CIA Friend," *Jerusalem Post,* December 5, 1987, is not online.
252. Cockburn, *Dangerous Liaison,* p. 44.

Chapter 6: Joe, the Cursed Peacemaker

253. Laurence Leamer, *Sons of Camelot: The Fate of an American Dynasty,* HarperCollins, 2005, kindle l. 262-267.
254. David Nasaw, *The Patriarch: The Remarkable Life and Turbulent Times of Joseph P. Kennedy,* Penguin Books, 2012, pp. 818-819.
255. Churchill's actual words were: "For my part, I consider that it will be found much better by all Parties to leave the past to history, especially as I propose to write that history."
256. A. J. P. Taylor in *The Origins of the Second World War* (1961), Penguin Books, 1991, kindle l. 384-396.

257. Michael R. Beschloss, *Kennedy and Roosevelt: The Uneasy Alliance,* Open Road, 1979, p.187.

258. James Douglass, *JFK and the Unspeakable: Why He Died and Why It Matters,* Touchstone, 2008, p. 21.

259. Nasaw, *The Patriarch,* p. 349.

260. Robert Caro, *The Years of Lyndon Johnson,* vol. IV: *The Passage of Power,* Alfred Knopf, 2012, p. 104. Also in Krock, *Memoirs,* p. 362.

261. In the journal of the *Herut,* Menachem Begin's political party, quoted in Alan Hart, *Zionism: The Real Enemy of the Jews,* vol. 2: *David Becomes Goliath,* Clarity Press, 2013, p. 252.

262. Seymour Hersh, *The Samson Option: Israel's Nuclear Arsenal and American Foreign Policy,* Random House, 1991, p. 96.

263. Hersh, *The Samson Option,* p. 103.

264. Edward Klein, *The Kennedy Curse: Why Tragedy Has Haunted America's First Family for 150 Years,* Saint Martin's Press, 2004.

265. Ronald Kessler, *The Sins of the Father: Joseph P. Kennedy and the Dynasty He Founded,* Coronet Books, 1997, quotes from the publisher's presentation and the back cover.

266. John Podhoretz, "A Conversation in Hell," *New York Post,* July 21, 1999, on nypost.com

267. Nasaw, *The Patriarch,* pp. 403-406.

268. Alan Hart, *Zionism: The Real Enemy of the Jews,* vol. 1: *The False Messiah,* Clarity Press, 2009, p. 164.

269. Clive Irving, "Joe Kennedy's answer to the Jewish question: ship them to Africa," Apr. 14, 2017, on www.thedailybeast.com

270. Avner Cohen, *Israel and the Bomb,* Columbia UP, 1998, pp. 10, 119.

271. Beschloss, *Kennedy and Roosevelt,* pp. 105-109.

272. Nasaw, *The Patriarch,* p. 373; also Beschloff, *Kennedy and Roosevelt,* p. 180.

273. Nasaw, *The Patriarch,* p. 396.

274. Beschloss, *Kennedy and Roosevelt,* pp. 185-186.

275. Beschloss, *Kennedy and Roosevelt,* p. 182.

276. Nasaw, *The Patriarch,* p. 425.

277. Nasaw, *The Patriarch,* p. 445.

278. Beschloss, *Kennedy and Roosevelt,* p. 199.

279. Beschloss, *Kennedy and Roosevelt,* p. 201.

280. Nasaw, *The Patriarch,* pp. 460-461. The quote is from Joe Kennedy's diary, according to David Irving, who renders it slightly differently in *Churchill's war,* vol. 1: *The Struggle for Power,* Focal Point, 2003, p. 207.

281. Nasaw, *The Patriarch,* p. 476.

282. Nasaw, *The Patriarch,* p. 496.

283. Nasaw, *The Patriarch,* p. 534.

284. David Irving, *Churchill's war,* vol. 1: *The Struggle for Power,* Focal Point, 2003, p. 207.

285. Beschloss, *Kennedy and Roosevelt,* pp. 15-16.

286. Beschloss, *Kennedy and Roosevelt,* pp. 43 and 230.

287. Beschloss, *Kennedy and Roosevelt,* pp. 235-237.

288. Beschloss, *Kennedy and Roosevelt,* p. 247.

289. Beschloss, *Kennedy and Roosevelt,* p. 273.

290. Nasaw, *The Patriarch,* p. 625; Beschloss, *Kennedy and Roosevelt,* p. 279.

291. Kessler, *The Sins of the Father,* p. 262.

292. Scott Farris, *Inga: Kennedy's Great Love, Hitler's Perfect Beauty, and J. Edgar Hoover's Prime Suspect,* Lyons Press, 2016.
293. Abigail Abrams, "Auction of Rare Diary Highlights What John F. Kennedy Really Thought About Hitler," *Time,* March 23, 2017, on time.com
294. Robert Taft, October 6, 1946, quoted in John F. Kennedy, *Profiles in Courage,* 1956, Harper Perennial, 2003, p. 199.
295. JFK to Ben Bradlee, quoted in Robert Kennedy, Jr., *American Values: Lessons I Learned from My Family,* HarperCollins, 2018, p. 101.
296. Arthur Schlesinger, *A Thousand Days: John Kennedy in the White House* (1965), Mariner Books, 2002, p. 88.
297. Christ Matthews, *Jack Kennedy, Elusive Hero,* Simon & Schuster, 2011, pp. 71-72.
298. Douglass, *JFK and the Unspeakable,* p. 5.
299. Quoted in Robert Kennedy, Jr., *American Values: Lessons I Learned from My Family,* HarperCollins, 2018, p. 101.
300. "Visit of Charles A. Lindbergh", on www.jfklibrary.org
301. Lynne Olson, *Those Angry Days: Roosevelt, Lindbergh, and America's Fight Over World War II, 1939-1941,* Random House, 2013.
302. Michael Collins Piper, *Final Judgment: The Missing Link in the JFK Assassination Conspiracy,* American Free Press, 6th ed., 2005, p. 117.
303. "The Umbrella Man", on Vimeo.com or YouTube
304. Patrick J. Buchanan, *Churchill, Hitler, and "The Unnecessary War": How Britain Lost Its Empire and the West Lost the World,* Crown Forum, 2008, p. 208.
305. Against the evidence, researchers John Simkin of Spartacus Educational and Russ Baker of WhoWhatWhy, have disputed that the umbrella was ever the symbol of Chamberlain.

Chapter 7: JFK Jr., the Slain Prince

306. The final report and the news release are both on www.ntsb.gov
307. Dale Russakoffand Lynne Duke, "JFK Jr.'s Joyful, Fateful Final Hours," *Washington Post,* July 21, 1999, on www.washingtonpost.com
308. Minibio on www.imdb.com/
309. Mark Walsh was the ideal witness of 9/11, with his famous line: "I saw this plane come out of nowhere and just ream right into the side of the Twin Tower exploding through to the other side, and then I witnessed both towers collapse, the first, and then the second, mostly due to structural failure because the fire was just too intense." Walsh happens to have worked for Fox TV interviewing him.
310. John Quinn, "Was JFK Jr Murdered?", August 2, 1999, on www.angelfire.com
311. Jeb Burnside, "Revisiting JFK, Jr.," *Aviation Safety Magazine,* June 2016, on www.aviationsafetymagazine.com
312. Listen to Jeffries's one-hour interview on midnightwriternews
313. Mitchell Zuckoff and Matthew Brelis, "Plane fell fast, probe finds," *Boston Globe,* July 20, 1999, on archive.boston.com
314. UPI article saved on www.whatreallyhappened.com. WCVB-TV repeated that information continuously during their first two days of reporting on the story. They broadcast, at 12:35 p.m. on July 17, a phone interview by anchor Susan Wornick of U.S. Coast Guard Petty Officer Todd Burgun, who confirmed the information.

315. Dave Saltonstall and Bill Hutchinson, "Angler May Have Heard Crash," *New York Daily News,* July 21, 1999, on nydailynews.com. Pribanic repeated his story to filmmaker Anthony Hilder.
316. Michael Zennie, "The Kennedys fought Over Where Bodies Would Be Buried…," *Daily Mail,* November 3, 2013, on www.dailymail.co.uk/
317. Dave Saltonstall, Austin Fenner, Helen Kennedy and Greg B. Smith, "John F. Kennedy Jr. went missing after taking a flight with his wife and her sister in 1999," *New York Daily News,* July 18, 1999, on nydailynews.com
318. Jackie's words reported by Pierre Salinger, quoted from Christopher Andersen, *The Good Son, JFK Jr. and the Mother He Loved,* Gallery Boosk, 2014, kindle l. 1912-4.
319. Christopher Andersen, *The Good Son, JFK Jr. and the Mother He Loved,* Gallery Boosk, 2014, kindle l. 1645-52.
320. Pierre Salinger, "Mourned for what he might have been," UPI, August 6, 1999, reproduced on www.orwelltoday.com/jfksalinger.shtml
321. Andersen, *The Good Son,* l. 1962-7.
322. Olivier Royant, *John, le dernier des Kennedy,* Éditions de l'Observatoire, 2018.
323. Andersen, *The Good Son,* l. 671-3
324. Andersen, *The Good Son,* l. 4300-4309
325. Andersen, *The Good Son,* l. 4808-11.
326. Read Robert D. McFadden's report on ia801309.us.archive.org
327. Liz McNeil, "Would JFK Jr. Have Run for President? His Best Friends Reveal His Last Days", July 19, 2016, people.com
328. Dominique Page, "Kennedy Junior: La pure hypothèse de l'assassinat," on largeur.com
329. Joe Siegel, "JFK Jr. Mulled Run For Senate in 2000," *New York Daily News,* July 20, 1999, on nydailynews.com
330. Liz McNeil, "Would JFK Jr. Have Run for President? His Best Friends Reveal His Last Days", July 19, 2016, on people.com
331. Matt Donnelly, "JFK Jr Would Have Run for President in 2016, Top Aide Says," *The Wrap,* July 29, 2016, on thewrap.com. Asked for *People magazine* if she tought JFK Jr. would have run for president, Terenzio answers: "I do think that eventually he would have made the leap" (on people.com at 3 minutes).
332. McNeil, "Would JFK Jr. Have Run for President?"
333. Gillon's interview on www.townandcountrymag.com
334. Joe Siegel, "JFK Jr. Mulled Run For Senate in 2000," *New York Daily News,* July 20, 1999, on nydailynews.com
335. Christopher Andersen, *The Good Son: JFK Jr. and the Mother He Loved,* Gallery Books, 2014, kindle l. 4918-44.
336. Read on Google.books. The audio recording of the book is on YouTube.
337. Andrew Collins, "Hillary Clinton & The Mysterious Death of JFK Jr.," May 8, 2016, on wjmiller.net/main1/?m=1-40
338. Quoted in John Koerner, *Exploding the Truth: The JFK Jr., Assassination,* Chronos Books, 2018, kindle l. 540-45.
339. Quoted in Koerner, *Exploding the Truth,* l. 540-5.
340. Jeffries's interview, "Donald Jeffries and the death of JFK Jr.", on midnightwriternews
341. Some researchers into JFK Jr.'s plane crash have suggested a connection to the TWA 800 crash, which happened three years earlier almost to the day, and in the same vicinity. Jackie Jura, author of Orwell Today website, wrote: "I remember when TWA 800 exploded and Salinger was going to give a press conference in Paris

to expose the truth. But then he cancelled it. The rumour on the net at the time was that the powers-that-be told him that if he gave the press conference they'd kill John-John, and so he backed down." Back down he did, but in May 27, 1999, he reiterated his claim, and John Jr. would die 50 days later(Jackie Jura, "Salinger True Kennedy Friend," on www.orwelltoday.com).
342. Guela Amir, "A Mother's Defense", *George,* March 1997, reproduced on groups.google.com
343. Jeffrey Salkin, "Will JFK's grandson become our first Jewish president?" Religion News Service, May 11, 2017, on religionnews.com/

Chapter 8: Forrestal, Kennedy's Foreshadow

344. Alan Hart, *Zionism: The Real Enemy of the Jews,* vol. 2: *David Becomes Goliath,* Clarity Press, 2013, p. 90.
345. Ronen Bergman, *Rise and Kill First: The Secret History of Israel's Targeted Assassinations*, Random House, 2018, p. 20.
346. It is now available on the Princeton University Library website in pdf form, or in HTML rendition by the anonymous Mark Hunter, who makes useful comments)
347. David Martin, *The Assassination of James Forrestal,* McCabe Publishing, 2019.
348. Charles Crenshaw, *JFK: Conspiracy of Silence,* 1992, quoted in James Douglass, *JFK and the Unspeakable: Why He Died and Why It Matters,* Touchstone, 2008, pp. 306-313. Dr Crenshaw kept silent for 30 years because, like so many others, he "reasoned that anyone who would go so far as to eliminate the President of the United States would surely not hesitate to kill a doctor" (p. 154). On the 21 other witnesses, Douglass, *JFK and the Unspeakable,* p. 283.
349. Martin, *The Assassination of James Forrestal,* p. 20
350. Truman Library: www.trumanlibrary.gov/library/oral-histories/leva
351. David Martin, "James Forrestal's 'Breakdown'," 23 June 2019, on www.dcdave.com
352. "Forrestal Out - Johnson In (1949)," on YouTube.
353. Truman Library: www.youtube.com/watch?v=E4tWrWhxJTk
354. John Loftus and Mark Aarons, *The Secret War against the Jews: How Western Espionage Betrayed The Jewish People,* St. Martin's Griffin, 2017, pp. 212-213.
355. Photos available on Mark Hunter's webpage ariwatch.com.
356. Both can be found on Mark Hunter's webpage ariwatch.com. Also on Martin's page www.dcdave.com
357. Martin, *The Assassination of James Forrestal,* p. 86.
358. Alfred Lilienthal, *What Price Israel?* (1953), Infinity Publishing, 2003, p. 50.
359. Martin, *The Assassination of James Forrestal,* pp. 52, 53, 87.

Conclusion

360. "Chomsky: Who cares who caused 9/11, who killed JFK. So many people die," on YouTube.
361. Yuri Slezkine, *The Jewish Century,* Princeton UP, 2004.
362. Lewis Richard Farnell, *Greek Hero Cults and Ideas of Immortality* (1921), Adamant Media Co., 2005, p. 343.
363. James DiEugenio, "The Posthumous Assassination of JFK", in *The Assassinations: Probe Magazine on JFK, MLK, RFK, and Malcolm X,* edited by Jim DiEugenio and Lisa Pease, Feral House, 2003.

364. Spartacus: spartacus-educational.com/JFKheymann.htm
365. Andrew Goldman, "Kennedy 'Expert' C. David Heymann: Do His J.F.K. Jr. Stories Hold Up?" *Observer,* August 2, 199, on observer.com; David Cay Johnston, "C. David Heymann's Lies About JFK and Jackie, Marilyn Monroe and Elizabeth Taylor", *Newsweek Magazine,* August 27, 2014, on www.newsweek.com
366. Robert Kennedy, Jr., *American Values: Lessons I Learned from My Family,* HarperCollins, 2018, p. 132.
367. Jim DeBrosse, *See No Evil: The JFK Assassination and the U.S. Media,* Trine Day, 2018. I quote from DeBrosse's PhD dissertation for Ohio University, 2014, on etd.ohiolink.edu/
368 Ari Shavit, "White Man's Burden," *Haaretz,* Apr 3, 2003, on www.haaretz.com
369. Strauss's "Introductory Essay" to Moses Maimonides, *The Guide to the Perplexed,* vol. 1, University of Chicago Press, 1963, pp. xiv-xv.
370. Leo Strauss, *Thoughts on Machiavelli,* University of Chicago Press, 1995, pp. 10-13.
371. "What Machiavelli (A Secret Jew?) Learned from Moses", *Jewish World Review,* June 7, 1999, on www.jewishworldreview.com
372. Leo Strauss, "Why we Remain Jews", quoted in Shadia Drury, *Leo Strauss and the American Right,* St. Martin's Press, 1999, pp. 31-43.
373. David Ben-Gurion and Amram Ducovny, *David Ben-Gurion, In His Own Words,* Fleet Press Corp., 1969, p. 116.
374. Dan Kurzman, *Ben-Gurion, Prophet of fire*, Olympic Marketing Corp, 1984, p. 26.
375. Herbert George Wells, *The Fate of Homo Sapiens*, 1939, p. 128.

Printed in Great Britain
by Amazon

83659736R00093